PRAISE FOR  JG

"Jefa in Training is a much-needed guide for all of us who need a blueprint to becoming a successful entrepreneur. Not only does this book provide the tools, but it provides the inspiration we all need to make that first step! Bravo, hermana!"

—**Eva Longoria**, award-winning actress, producer, director, activist, philanthropist, and CEO of UnbeliEVAble Entertainment

"A great roadmap for a new generation of Latinas who are looking to start an entrepreneurial journey!"

—**Gaby Natale**, three-time Daytime Emmy award-winning entrepreneur, author, and motivational speaker

"Jefa In Training by Ashley K. Stoyanov Ojeda is a gift to the Latino and bilingual community of women who are ready to make their entrepreneurial dreams a reality. Gracias madrina!"

—**Fernanda Kelly**, Emmy award-winning actress/activist, founder and CEO of NYTAQ

"The Hispanic community is the fastest-growing, largest, and youngest cohort in America. Latinas are at the heart of that growth and the time is now for our community to shine. All 30 million Latinas should feel equipped and empowered to be Jefas and in the driver's seat. The more tools and guidance we can provide for Latinas to grow and shine, the faster we can get there. Bravo, *Jefa in Training.* #hispanocstar #Togetherweshine!"

—**Claudia Romo Edelman**, diplomat, communication strategist and special adviser for the United Nations and We Are All Human Foundation

"Educational, relatable, and inspirational! *Jefa in Training* provides you with powerful tools you need to kickstart your entrepreneurial journey. It also gives you that push para seguir adelante!"

—**Tania Torres**, MBA, business coach and co-founder of Latina Approved

"*Jefa in Training* is exactly the type of book I would have wanted at the start of my entrepreneurial journey. It's an incredible gift for the next generation of Latinas ready to become their own Jefas. The step-by-step advice is on point, with very specific action steps on how to build a successful business. The best part is how Ashley K. Stoyanov Ojeda does it perfectly 'in culture.' "

—**Beatriz Acevedo**, CEO and co-founder of We Are Suma and Somos Suma, president of Acevedo Foundation

"Latina-owned small businesses are the fastest-growing segment in business, yet we lack accessible resources for our community. *Jefa In Training* delivers the resources and necessary guidance, chapter by chapter, that break down the fundamentals of business development for Latina entrepreneurs from the perspective of successful Latina founders."

—**Marivette Navarrete**, founder/CEO of The Mujerista

"Ashley has brought a culturally competent guide to all aspiring jefas. Her real-life experiences coupled with proven strategies gives us Latinas a guide we can truly relate to. My personal work with Ashley has helped me grow my business, and now other mujeres will have the amazing opportunity to do the same!"

—**Alejandra Aguirre**, co-founder/owner of Cadena Collective

"When a mujer is paving her own path to success, there is nothing more powerful than seeing someone who looks like her beating the odds and in the position that she aspires to be one day. Representation matters, and Ashley is the resilient leader that our community is fortunate enough to learn from."

—**Estrella Serrato**, founder, podcast host of *Cafecito con Estrellita*, daughter of immigrants, and graduate student

"Creating the path to your dream career isn't always simple, but Ashley is a guide who will light the way. Through thoughtful prompts, case studies, and easy-to-follow advice, *Jefa in Training* will equip you with the tools to successfully build a connection between your cultura, ambition, and goals."
—**Zameena Mejia**, freelance writer at *Latina*

"This book is for ordinary womxn with an extraordinary idea and limited resources. It's for the person who counts themselves out before they even step in the game. It's for anyone who dares to dream yet is too afraid to act. *Jefa in Training* is the business coach + mentor new entrepreneurs need and can't afford in early stages. Do not let go of your potential; get disciplined using this book and its real stories to remind you of what is possible."
—**Kalima DeSuze,** owner of Cafe con Libros, an intersectional feminist bookstore and coffee shop

"This is the business guide I wished I had twelve years ago when I first started my entrepreneurial journey... May *Jefa in Training* be the blueprint that opens the path for many more successful businesses founded by Latinas!"
—**Ana Flores**, founder of WeAllGrow Latina

Jefa

in training

Jefa
in training

The Business Startup Toolkit for Entrepreneurial and Creative Women

Ashley K. Stoyanov Ojeda

FIU | Business Press
FLORIDA INTERNATIONAL UNIVERSITY

Cover Design: Elina Diaz
Cover Photo/illustration: madiwaso.stock.adobe.com
Layout & Design: Elina Diaz

For permission requests, please contact the publisher at:
Mango Publishing Group
2850 S Douglas Road, 4th Floor
Coral Gables, FL 33134 USA
info@mango.bz

For special orders, quantity sales, course adoptions and corporate sales, please email the publisher at sales@mango.bz. For trade and wholesale sales, please contact Ingram Publisher Services at customer.service@ingramcontent.com or +1.800.509.4887.

Jefa in Training: The Business Startup Toolkit for Entrepreneurial and Creative Women

Library of Congress Cataloging-in-Publication number: 2021947518
ISBN: (print) 978-1-64250-729-4, (ebook) 978-1-64250-730-0
BISAC category code BUS025000, BUSINESS & ECONOMICS / Entrepreneurship

Printed in the United States of America

Dedicated to
the original jefas who continue to inspire me
every day desde el cielo.
This is for you, Abuelita Rosalina Ojeda Aburto
and Meme Denise Kervabon.

Table of Contents

Introducción

¡Adelante!

Welcome to your roadmap to entrepreneurship. It is a magical place to be—and you belong here.

If you feel like you want to start a business but do not know what kind of business—*adelante*! If you have started building your business but don't know how to take the next steps—*adelante*! If you're looking for strategies and inspiration from experienced entrepreneurs to take your business to the next level—*adelante*!

My name is Ashley, and I am here to be your hada madrina of business for the next twelve chapters—and as fairy godmothers do, I'm going to guide you through this new journey of yours. From homing in on your idea to implementing sales strategies, from building a community to becoming a thought leader in your industry—this book is made to help you launch.

At the beginning of 2020, right when the world was just starting to shut down due to COVID-19, I started working with Marivette Navarrete, the founder of *The Mujerista*, a digital publication empowering and celebrating the next generation of Latinas, to build and grow the organization's first ever online network. We started hosting weekly Zoom meetups to discuss the struggles of our businesses during the shutdown. For the next three months, we continued to build upon these meetups until our membership was ready to launch. Since then, I've

Jefa in Training

helped provide hundreds of women with the resources to help launch their creative projects and navigate all the ups and downs of being a founder.

The Mujerista community needed a trusted resource during a pivotal time in its unfolding. For my part, I felt I'd finally found the community I'd been looking for since starting my journey as a socialpreneur in 2016—one that understood how our upbringings shape us as business professionals and how our Latinidad and generational status give us a unique perspective on the world. We found comfort in each other because we were all finding our way through entrepreneurship. We could relate to each other's cultural backgrounds and values and how they had helped us become who we are today.

You see, when I first fell into the world of entrepreneurship, I looked to every book and blog out there—and while most of what I found was great, all of what I found was written by someone who had little in common with me. Some material would stick, but sometimes nothing would resonate and I would find myself wondering if there was something wrong with me. I longed to connect with experienced founders who knew what it was like to grow up in a lower middle-class family. I searched for other women business owners who were also the first in their family to go to college. Where were all the other women who wanted to break out of the nine-to-five, who also split their time between the states and visiting their family in Latin America? I did not find that community until The Mujerista Network was born. Being around other Latinas building beautiful, impactful businesses felt natural and somehow gave me the same feeling of belonging I felt every summer when I would reunite with my primos en Mexico. It felt like home. And that is what I want this book to feel like for you.

There is a lack of representation in publishing, in media, in tech, in music, and in business, and because of that, so many women, especially women of color and first-gen entrepreneurs, feel like they don't have a shot at building something great—something that can create change, something that can create generational wealth. If there is anything you get from this book, I hope it's the inspiration and confidence that you too can move forward with your ideas.

If you feel like you don't have the experience, the funding, or the support system to realize your entrepreneurial dreams, know that you're not alone. I know what it's like to ask yourself all of the what-if questions and feel like you aren't getting anywhere. Those voices were in my head too, telling me all kinds of things as I worked to launch my first organization.

But I also had mi mami and mis abuelitas whom I could call in moments of overwhelm, and they would tell me, "*Sí se puede!*" I am so happy I listened to them, because taking that leap and replacing "What if I fail?" with "What could be achieved if I try?" has changed my life in more ways than I could have ever imagined.

Para Más Inspiración: Mi Historia

How a Showcase Turned into a Movement

In 2015, I was an aspiring singer-songwriter looking to find herself after graduating college; I made a move from New York City to Portland, Oregon, with no intention of starting a business, just simply looking for a creative community to collaborate with after my arrival. At the time, the Portland music industry was scattered, and while there was an abundance of talent in the city, there was a lack of cultural infrastructure to support it, and when my favorite (though short-lived) open mic shut down, I was at a loss as to how to advance my career in my new city.

A few months later, I saw an opportunity to host an ongoing showcase at a local venue where I could start to create the community I so desperately wanted and needed. And so, I launched a monthly series to showcase the best rising women songwriters in the city. Within three months of launching the series, I had artists approaching me from all over the city, local media started coming and covering the shows, and soon enough, booking agents and other industry professionals began attending the showcases to scout for talent. In Portland, my monthly showcase had become not only a community initiative but a place for these artists to make the connections they needed to level up their careers. Still, I wanted to do more.

I was not sure what the next step was, so I started reaching out for advice to various women in music groups I was a part of. Instead of getting advice about how to grow this local showcase, I had requests to expand it to other cities. That's when I felt the spark—a lightbulb went off in my head, and I realized that growing this initiative was no longer about me. This need for an online community where rising women songwriters around the country could collaborate and share resources with each other went far beyond what would serve me personally.

Fast forward a year, and I was building little teams to host monthly showcases, workshops, and networking events in New York City, Nashville, and Vancouver. As I saw interest rising, I also felt a little panic: I had no idea what to do next. I knew what I wanted to offer our community, but I could not figure out what to call what we were doing. Had I started a booking agency? Had I started an artist management company? When people would ask, I would tell them, "I just want to help." After a few months of talking to mentors in the industry, I made the decision to make the community a nonprofit. That way, I could grow the organization and impact as many people as possible. And that was just the beginning.

The tiny local showcase that started at a venue with a forty-person cap, driven by a need to connect with like-minded individuals, has now grown into an international community of over ten thousand rising women and nonbinary songwriters. We have connected European and South American songwriters, been featured by The Recording Academy, and partnered with top industry companies like CD Baby and Elektra Records to host educational webinars. Our songwriters have been picked up by sync licensing companies and have gone on to open for bigger artists.

Unintentionally, I started a movement. And it has been one hell of a ride.

Being a founder has been a journey, a journey filled with ups and downs and moments of both extreme pride and extreme panic. It has also been a never-ending crash course—a series of lessons on what to do, what I could have done better, and what I should not have done at all. Until I launched this project, I knew nothing about best practices for building a foundation, a community, cold-pitching, or thought leadership, etc. What I never imagined was how fast it would grow, or that it would only be the beginning of my journey in business. Since starting #WCM, I have teamed up with startup and corporate tech companies to help build their communities and develop their businesses. And all of it has led to this very moment—now it's time for me to pass those lessons along to you.

That brings us back to the purpose of this book: to help you navigate through the beginning phases of launching your passion-filled business, side hustle, project—you name it. This is your very own toolkit that you can write in, highlight, and use in whatever way you think will be most helpful to build the foundation of what you want to pursue.

Each lesson will include fill-in prompts, checklists, a worksheet, and insights from other Latina founders to help lead the way. The steps and framework you need to launch your business are here for you so you can start today and then check back in for a refresher down the line.

The beginning of my entrepreneurial journey taught me many things, but the first thing I want to pass along to you is this: If you feel there is a need for something, chances are, you are not the only one.

So let's go and figure out the rest! Buena suerte, jefas.

Your training begins ahora.

¡Adelante!
Ashley K. Stoyanov Ojeda

"¡Pies para que los quiero si tengo alas para volar?"

—Frida Kahlo

Lección 1

Pa' Empezar

Para empezar, congratulations on taking the first step in your entrepreneurial journey! Whether you have a million ideas for a project or are struggling to really nail one down—this chapter es para ti! The first step in launching or growing anything is, well, figuring out what that something is.

If you have picked up this book, it is likely that you have been wanting to launch a creative project or business—or maybe you have many ideas and get overwhelmed by the hundreds of things running through your head (*trust me*, I have been there). In this first chapter, we're not only going to go through how to develop your idea, but also how to validate that your idea is worth pursuing.

Consider this first chapter as the pre-work you'll need before you can build your brand and put together your sales strategy. If you've been sitting on an idea for a while and truly believe in it, this chapter will help you go deeper with your market research to better identify your target audience and competitors. After learning everything you can about your market, the Brain Dump exercise at the end of this chapter will help you tie things up before heading into constructing your foundation.

How to Home in on Your Idea

It takes an incredible amount of energy to really home in on an idea and start to move the needle forward in developing it—especially for multi-passionate entrepreneurs who can see themselves doing a lot of different things throughout their lifetime. It is a problem that I have faced, and chances are, if you have a creative rather than technical mindset, you can relate.

From having started out in the music industry to currently developing startups and helping creatives launch businesses, along the way I realized that though my roles and industries changed, the reason why I was doing these things has not. My personal "why" has always been to create opportunities for underrepresented entrepreneurs and creatives. No matter what I do next, that will always be at the center of it.

If your question is "but how do I find my personal *why*?" the answer is to find out what fuels it.

For myself and many others, it is personal. Growing up in a big city, trying to break into music and entrepreneurship as a daughter of an immigrant and as a woman in all male-dominated fields, coming from a lower middle-class family, I felt that I had few resources to show me the way and even fewer I could trust to help me get to where I wanted to be. Now that I have connections after having been lucky enough to be given opportunities to accelerate my career, I want to be able to do that in turn for people who grew up like me. Your "why" may be motivated by something similar—a yearning for something different, a need for change.

Jefa in Training

A quote that has stuck with me is one by Arlan Hamilton from her book, *It's About Damn Time:*

> *If you close your eyes and visualize the world five, ten, twenty years from now and feel okay with the thing you're working on not existing, then it's not urgent. But if you can't imagine the world without it and want it to exist whether you get to enjoy the benefits of it or not, then not only is it important to you, it is your calling.*

Your "why" is the power behind your business. Your purpose is what is going to help build your product, what will fuel your marketing, and what will motivate people to help you grow. Whatever it is, it will be the foundation upon which you will build what will end up being your business's mission.

Para Más Inspiración: Un Ejemplo
Finding Your "Why" With Stephanie and Melissa Carcache

Mis amigas, singer/songwriter Stephanie and actress Melissa Carcache, are sisters as well as founders of the number one podcast for millennial women, *Millennial Women Talk*. They are creative influencers who were first inspired to launch their entrepreneurial journey by watching their Cuban parents run their small business in Miami, Florida. Now, both sisters run their own artistic careers while still helping their family strengthen the family businesses.

"All we saw growing up was entrepreneurship. When the Cubans came to Miami, many people and places rejected them. I still remember old photos of shops in Miami Beach that would hang signs outside their doors that said, 'No Cubans.' But the amazing thing to me was how the lack of opportunity directed at them was the fire that made them create their own opportunities! They said, 'Well, if I am not allowed in this shop, then I will just build my own shop!' And that is the mentality we grew up around."

—Stephanie Carcache

Inspired by how both their parents and the wider Cuban community have created their own spaces in Miami, they're now creating spaces where they can be represented in the arts and media industries. If you are struggling between a few different ideas, think about their journey. Try making a list of causes you advocate for, things you have taken up as hobbies throughout your life, meaningful experiences that have influenced you, and of course, tu cultura!

_____

_____

_____

_____

_____

_____

Jefa in Training

How to Know if Your Idea Is a Good Idea

No hay que tenerle miedo a nuestras ideas. But the key is in knowing how to break them down and become very familiar with the market—and that is exactly what we are going to do in this next step.

Before we get too excited and start building out further plans for your idea, remember that knowledge is power, which is why now is the time to learn everything you can about what you are going to be launching. Many businesses fail because they do not know if there is enough demand for what they plan to offer or the buying power of those whom they are targeting. Therefore, the most important step you can take at this point in your journey is research—specifically, market research.

What Is Market Research?

Market research is an essential part of the process for any launch. Here, you will learn the ins and outs of your industry and audience. This is time-consuming; it may not be fun, but it is necessary and may save you from facing avoidable challenges in the future. Thankfully, we live in the time of Google, and we can find practically anything and everything in the world of information right at our fingertips.

In case you need a head start on what methods to use, here are a few ways you can go about doing it:

Use a Market Research Database

Market research databases can give you accurate information about your competitors and target audience. By using these databases, you will be able to learn more about your industry and level up your position before you even get started. You will also get insight on potential opportunities, and with this information, you may even be able to minimize investment risks. Recommended databases include: the Census Bureau, Statista.com, Alexa's Audience Overlap Tool, and Google Trends.

Talk to Your Ideal Customer

Figuring out who your target audience is and approaching them directly can pinpoint their true pain points, expectations, and goals, and in turn, can help you refine your product/service offerings. This can also help you prioritize, especially if you are wondering what to launch first!

Start with a survey: First ask them to fill out a short survey, one that won't take up a lot of their time but can still give you valuable information. If you want to create surveys, you can use Google Surveys or the SurveyMonkey web page to start.

Some important things to ask include:

- General demographic information (age, location, occupation)
- How are they currently dealing with the need you are hoping to fill?
- If they are happy with this solution—what is their budget for something like what you are offering?

- How do they receive news and/or find out about new brands offering this product or service (social media and ads, emails, word of mouth)?

- If they are currently paying for a product service, what needs are not being met?

- If they are not currently spending to fill this need, what exactly are they looking for? The more specific the better.

Interview them one-on-one: Surveys are great, but generally they are just a starting point. Talking to potential customers one-on-one will not only allow you to ask more in-depth questions and leave room for follow-ups, it will also create the opportunity for you to initiate a genuine connection with them. These are people that you will be able to keep in the loop about the progress of your business—you can invite them to be part of your launch, and with luck, they can one day become ambassadors for you as you grow.

Talk to Other Industry Leaders

Talking to other leaders in your industry who serve the same audience with which you hope to connect can be beneficial as they will have more experience with and knowledge of the pain points and interests of your new target audience. They may also be open to partnering with you or connecting you to someone who can help down the line. It's always good to get different perspectives on what you are building, especially from people in your industry who have done it before. Who are the leaders in your field whom you admire? It never hurts to reach out to see if they have fifteen minutes to chat with you about your idea. They can be a huge resource to help familiarize you with unique aspects of the landscape, such as expected growth rates and potential unfilled

needs in your industry. It is also likely that they can connect you to other people and resources.

Identify and Analyze Competitors

Research any competitors who are selling similar products and/ or services and who have a similar style. A great way to do this is to conduct a competitive analysis. A competitive analysis can be done in many forms, but in general, it acts as a comparison of your competitors' services, products, and strategies. This is a great thing to do early on in your business research so you can find out what holes might need to be filled in your industry.

Here are some of the major elements that you can include when you do an analysis of the competition:

- Who are their target customers?

- What services and/or products do they provide?

- What are their price points for their products or services?

- Do they have funding from outside their business?

- What is their website like? Is it image-heavy? Does it get their message across? How? Do they have enough calls to action? Too many?

- From the moment you go to their website to when you are prompted to subscribe to a newsletter or see an ad, what is their customer experience like? What is their customer support like?

- How are they marketing themselves? Where do they get most of their traction? Blog shares? Newsletter? Social media?

- What is their communication flow like? How many emails do you get from them and when?

- ❱ How do they encourage customer loyalty? Referral programs? Brand ambassadors?

- ❱ What are people saying about them? Are they getting press features? What do current customers say?

- ❱ What do they claim is their Unique Selling Proposition (USP)?

Your answers will not only help you build your foundation but will also serve as solid validation—they will verify that there is a need both for what you are creating now and what you will go on to create in the future. In Chapter Six, we'll go into how to use this information to develop your Unique Selling Proposition, but doing this exercise now for five competitors in your field will give you a great head start.

Market research is essential before you continue the planning process, but its importance does not end once you have launched! Staying in the loop on trends will also help you develop the tone you use to communicate with your brand's followers, how you set your prices, and ways to keep your customers happy, as well as provide clarity when you need to decide what services or products to launch further down the line.

~~~~~~

Key Takeaways from Lección 1

If you feel there is a need for something, chances are you are not the only one.

- ❱ Identify your target audience as soon as you can; doing so will help guide you to do the research you need for your launch and solidify your foundation early on.

- ❱ Do the research:

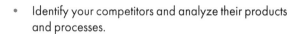

- Identify your competitors and analyze their products and processes.

- Talk to your dream customers; have them take surveys or interview them one-on-one.

▶ Stay on top of trends in your industry—market research for your business does not end when you launch.

Nailing down a business idea is the very first step in building your foundation; think of what we are doing right now as your business blueprint. Blueprints are the initial visualization; mix them with some strategy, tools, and patience, and you'll have a solid foundation on which to build.

With all of the inspiración y información from the first chapter in mind: what is your idea, jefa? It is time to figure it all out in this chapter's worksheet.

¡Manos a la Obra!

Brain Dump

List all the current ideas you have, even if they seem crazy or out of reach. And if you need some direction, try answering the following:

What do you enjoy doing? What are you passionate about?

_____

_____

What are you knowledgeable about?

_____

_____

What need(s) do you want to fill?

_____

_____

Do you want to sell a service or a product?

_____

_____

Do you want to do something virtually, or do you prefer to create something that requires being in a physical space?

_____

_____

Once you have answered those, take your answers a step further and for each of them, answer these:

- ❏ Can you roughly envision various ways to monetize it?

- ❏ Will it still be relevant in the next year? In the next three years?

- ❏ Will there be enough of a demand for your product or service to sustain your making a living?

☐ Is it something that you can see yourself successfully scaling up?

If you have answered no to the last set of questions, start crossing your original ideas out and try the exercise again. Whether your idea is to launch the next best podcast or to be the next woman to have her company go public, failing to think through these four questions could be what sinks you before you even begin.

Once you have answered those, get a start on your market research! Here are some questions to get you going:

Is the market big enough for the business you envision? How many potential customers are out there?

_____

_____

Do you see this market growing in the next three years?

_____

_____

Use this chart to do your first round of competitive analysis for three competitors. Reference this information as you continue to build your foundation.

Jefa in Training

Competitor	Target Audience	What do they offer

Price points	Marketing Strategy	Customer Experience

Communication Flow	What are other people saying	Other notes

"Los sueños
no se cumplen,
se trabajan."

-Mia Pineda

Lección 2

A Construir

What business will you be developing throughout the rest of this book?

_____

Now that you have your idea and have done some research, let's start building your foundation. In this chapter, we're going to dive into crafting your mission, vision, and values. These are the very beginning pieces of the puzzle, and they will help guide you through the rest of the planning process. Once you have these pieces, the next steps in the chapter will lead you to creating your very first set of business goals.

You will learn two different frameworks for setting goals for your business, learn some best practices from Tania Torres, founder of Latina Boss Academy, and then make a timeline for the next three months.

Let's jump in.

Building Your Foundation

The basis of every business or project will be its mission, and what will guide you will ultimately be your vision.

La Misión

Your mission defines your business and the approach you will use to reach your goals. This is what outsiders will see when they decide whether or not to work with you or buy from you. This is a necessary part of beginning to build your brand (and if you are a solopreneur, yes, you *are* the brand), so making it as clear as possible is especially important. Think about what is important to your potential clients/consumers/followers and make sure that is in your mission statement.

While drafting your mission, it should state the following:

- What you do
- How you do it
- Who you do it for
- And as a bonus: what *value* you bring (that others do not). We will come back to this and do a deep dive into your Unique Selling Proposition in a later chapter.

La Visión

Your vision describes the goal of your company (i.e., what you want to achieve). Some people call it a roadmap since it defines where you may want a brand to be within a certain timeframe. At its core, though, your vision should be what inspires you to keep moving forward.

While your personal "why" might be what has inspired the mission of your business, your business vision should not only share that "why" (your personal purpose) but also the impact you hope to have in the future. If you conducted market research and did competitive analysis in the last chapter, did you find anything important about what is missing in your industry? Use whatever is motivating you to find a solution for this or create something to help to formulate your vision. Even if it seems a bit far away from what you'll do in the beginning, your vision is exactly what the word says it is. This is what will drive your clients to be loyal to you and refer people to you. It might in the end be what sets you apart from everyone else.

Regardless of whether your long-term goal is to one day have a thousand employees or to move forward as a solopreneur forever (or something as yet undefined), your vision has to be uniquely true to you and must resonate with your story.

~~~~~~

Para Más Inspiración: Un Ejemplo
Crafting a Powerful Vision like Bianca Kea

Bianca Kea, founder of Yo Soy Afro Latina, felt a need to create a community. That is how her brand was born.

Check out her website to learn more about her inspiring vision; here is her mission statement as an example of clearly articulated values:

> **The Mission:** At Yo Soy Afro Latina, we are on a mission to empower Black women within the Latin community. Founded by a Black woman, YSAL celebrates Afro-Latinidad in the Americas,

and we are here to validate our hermanas' experience. This is more than a trend or a movement. This is a celebration of a culture that is just as diverse as it is rich in pride.

The Vision: My goal is to shed light on the beauty and the magnitude of Afro Latinas, to create a space where we are acknowledged, and to celebrate our beautiful, diverse culture. We have been here, and we're not going anywhere. This is our time to shine.

Can you start to see how your mission and vision will be different yet connected? Having a clear and concise mission and vision is important when working to connect with your future supporters.

If you cannot connect with your idea beyond your mission to create a vision, it is possible that seed is not yet ready to be planted, because if you cannot see its further unfolding, other people will not either. If that is the case, go back to Lección 1 and redo your brain dump. This is a normal part of the foundation-building process, which is why we take this time to craft our vision.

Values

Your business is heavily built on what you have defined in your mission and vision as well as on the values you decide are important to you and your company's culture. You will be able to look back on these when crafting any part of your brand; we will go more into detail on that in the next chapter.

Setting brand values that are in line with your vision and mission will help you genuinely connect with your audience down the line. What is important to you?

Some examples of brand values are:

- Integrity
- Honesty
- Creativity
- Passion
- Accountability
- Diversity
- Impact
- Leadership
- Mindfulness
- Devotion
- Teamwork

Your values should be easy to remember, so you do not want to pick more than ten.

Did any of these resonate with you? Jot some initial ideas down here.

Brand values are not something to be taken lightly as they, along with your vision, will shine a guiding light as you move further along in your journey as a jefa. When you are forced to make important decisions, when you are looking for like-minded companies to collaborate with, you will look to your values to provide a reminder of what your brand is all about.

Setting Goals

Your thoughts are likely running a million miles a minute right now, and that is okay. It is easy to feel like you're being split into a million different directions at once; that is why it is important to set goals. Especially in the beginning, you will have to evaluate and reevaluate how and when you do certain things. This is completely normal and will also bring positive results.

~~~~~~

Para Más Inspiración: Unos Consejos
Three Tips for Goal-Setting from Tania Torres

Before we go into learning how to use a goal-setting framework and start putting pen to paper, I want to share some wisdom from Tania Torres, entrepreneur, business coach, and content creator. She is the founder of Latina Boss Academy, an online platform that helps women discover their superpowers and teaches them about entrepreneurship. Tania also created and hosts the podcast *All Things Latina*, where she educates thousands of women every month about business and career matters. She is also cofounder of Latina Approved, a digital lifestyle brand that inspires and empowers Latinas every day.

Tania has some powerfully useful knowledge to share on how focused goal setting is key to developing a successful business.

Set Short-Term and Long-Term Goals.

Define the "why" of your goal and whether it is for the short or long term. Dissect why you want to reach this goal. Once you discover the "why," it will help you stay on track to reach it.

Jefa in Training

Match Each Goal with an Action Step.

For example, if you say you want to improve your public speaking skills, then you might want to take a public speaking class or practice speaking in small groups until you are ready to speak in a larger group.

Don't Just Set Goals, Have a Timeline.

It is crucial that you set up a timeline for when you want to accomplish this goal. Set deadlines, as this will help you stay organized and prioritize what you need to accomplish.

~~~~~~

As Tania mentions, setting timelines with action steps is crucial to advancing your idea. For this chapter's ejercicio, you will be putting all of what you have learned thus far into setting yourself up for your launch with a SWOT Analysis, learning how to define SMART goals, and then finally, putting your goals for the next three months down on paper!

Listas?

Step 1: Do a SWOT Analysis

A great way to start off your goal setting process is to do a SWOT Analysis. A SWOT Analysis is a simple but effective framework for strategic planning in which you assess **Strengths**, **Weaknesses**, **Opportunities**, and **Threats** in relation to your business or project.

In the Strengths section, you'll write down not only the things that you do particularly well, but also the things that you bring to the table that your competitors won't. It could be your mix of experiences, your network and reach, access to low-cost production, or other pluses—anything that gives you a clear advantage.

When analyzing Weaknesses, you'll be forced to take a look at what skills or resources you may be lacking. It's important to be realistic here and maybe even take this time to ask for feedback from a trusted group of mentors or friends in your industry. Sometimes we can be blind to what we need to improve.

Under Opportunities, you'll write down any trends you see coming up that will help launch your idea. Opportunities are things that aren't always within your control to create, but it will be up to you to try and take advantage of them when they appear! Think about: bigger brands looking for partners or grants opening up around a certain time of year.

In the Threats section, include anything that may negatively impact what you're building: a new competitor launching soon, potential delays in shipping because of USPS problems, or a partner you had lined up pulling the plug on your plans. These are all things that could affect your flow, and you'll want to think about alternative solutions if these situations arise.

Strengths	Weaknesses
_____	_____
_____	_____
_____	_____
_____	_____
Opportunities	**Threats**
_____	_____
_____	_____
_____	_____
_____	_____

You might be wondering, *but how do I use a SWOT Analysis to put together goals?* Entrepreneurship is a journey of endless growth, and doing a SWOT Analysis can help you see that perhaps you can use some of your strengths to take advantage of opportunities. If you can learn to take your vulnerabilities and shift your approach in a way that transforms them into strengths, it will open up surprising opportunities. Pivot weaknesses by bringing in new resources, for instance, by upgrading your skills or outsourcing.

Step 2: Practice Writing Your Goals and Make Them SMART

SMART is not just a cute acronym, it is a tool to help you gain clarity—one to keep in mind when putting pen to paper. Get a jump on your prelaunch preparations by keeping each of these elements in mind when setting goals!

Specific: Being specific will help you stay focused on what is simple and relevant. Ask yourself the who, what, where, when, and why of your goal.

Measurable: You'll need to be able to say how you will know if this goal has been accomplished. Is it a certain number of clients you need to bring on board? A percentage of sales from referrals? A certain number of downloads of your free content? Note how you will measure progress. This will keep you motivated!

Achievable: Do you already have the skills and resources to accomplish this goal? If it seems like a stretch, consider taking a step back and making the moves you need to make in order to become more fully prepared to move forward.

Relevant: Make sure your goals are reasonable in relation to where you are in your journey! Also think about how the steps needed to get to these goals relate to the rest of what you have going on. For example, if one of your goals is to take a digital marketing course but you know you already have a lot going on, it may not be a very relevant or realistic goal at present.

Time-Based: Give yourself a deadline for all of your goals. Check in with yourself to make sure the deadlines you set are realistic, and don't let anything get in the way! Join an accountability group and let them know what your goals are so they can help keep you on track.

Key Takeaways from Lección 2

Your mission defines your business and your chosen approach to reach your goals.

▶ Your vision describes the goal of your company (i.e., what you want to achieve).

▶ Both your mission and vision will be the basis of the brand you are building.

▶ Entrepreneurship is a journey of endless growth. Think about your Strengths, Weaknesses, and Opportunities, as well as potential Threats to your business. Doing a SWOT Analysis can help you see that perhaps you can use some of your strengths to take advantage of opportunities.

▶ It's easy to feel like you're being split into a million different directions at once, and that is why it is important to set goals—specific, measurable, achievable, relevant, and time-based goals.

▶ Hold yourself accountable for your goals—stay consistent and track any changes.

Keeping all of this in mind, now it's time to set your goals! The following worksheet will help you put these down on paper before we move on to our next lesson, which is all about creating your brand.

¡Manos a la Obra!

Goal-Setting Worksheet

This worksheet's purpose is to help you work out your goals for the next three months. You may want to keep this handy as you go through the book so you can add more things to your to-do list.

Here is an example of a SMART goal that might be relevant to you:

Goal 1: Have a website up and running in the next two months for my project.

A. Define mission and vision by next week.
B. Write out a bio in two weeks.
C. Hire a photographer for headshots and/or product shots for a shoot in three weeks.
D. Pick a domain name and register it in four weeks.
E. Pick out colors and layout in five weeks.

Your turn! Fill out the following chart and plug in your timeline on the next page!

GOAL	STEPS	DEADLINE

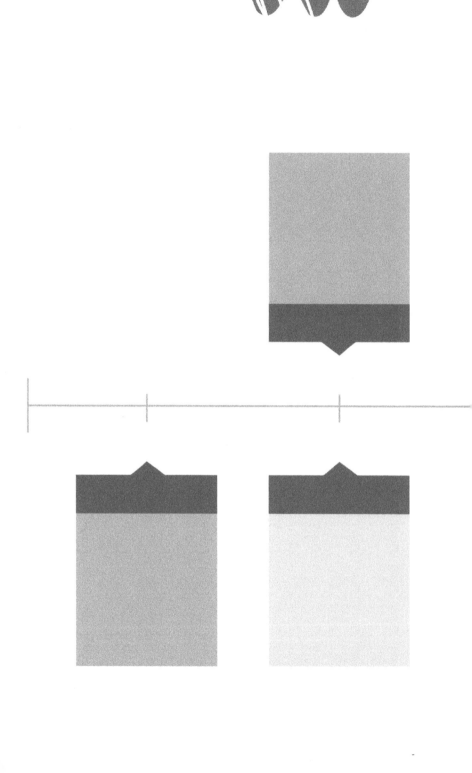

"Puedes ser mil mujeres diferentes. Tú decides cuál quieres ser."

—Salma Hayek

Lección 3

A Crear

Creating Your Brand

Remember when I said that your mission and vision will be the basis of, well, *everything*? Now it's time to put that into practice! In this chapter, we'll be focusing on the creation of your brand. From developing your brand's identity on through your business' name, aesthetic, messaging, to putting it all together, this chapter will equip you with the tools to start creating the assets you need to move forward.

But first, let's define the key word in this chapter: *Brand*.

What Is a Brand Anyway?

Can't we just attach a cute logo to our idea and call it a day? If only it were that simple!

Here is the definition of a brand according to the American Marketing Association: A brand is a name, term, design, symbol, or any other feature that identifies one seller's goods or services as distinct from those of other sellers.

My in-depth definition: Your brand will encompass everything—the colors you use to represent yourself, the tone you employ when communicating with your followers, the partners with whom you align yourself, and the ideas that you stand behind. Your brand is what you want people to say about you.

Developing Your Brand's Identity

Having a strong brand identity is not only important to connect with future customers, but to make your business recognizable and distinct from your competitors. In this section, we'll go through a checklist of the different components of your brand's identity and why each of them is important. Once you are done with the checklist, the face of your brand will be ready to share with the world. The goal is this: based on how you represent your brand, when people look for the expert or top seller in your industry, they think of you.

Your brand's identity will encompass the following things:

YOUR NAME

A brand's name is its main identifier, and while there is no formula for how to name your brand, you'll want to make sure it's easy for people to remember (and if the name is too long, maybe you'll want your business to be known by an acronym). Think about what you will be offering and how you'll be offering it. Your name can also tell a story or include your values.

For example: "The Honest Company" was built on Jessica Alba's strong beliefs in transparency and honesty in business; therefore, she built her business name, mission, and vision around those values.

Para Más Inspiración: Un Tip
Haz Un Name Check!

Once you have a name or two in mind, you will want to make sure what you choose is not already trademarked and that the web domain name and social media handles are available. Remember that not only will your website be associated with this, but also your business' email address, social media handles, and more, so you should ensure that you have complete ownership of the ones you'll need.

Here are a few places to check to make sure you're able to use the name you have in mind.

- ✧ **Google and Social Media:** Doing a comprehensive search before you go and search for verification on state and federal sites could be helpful. Type in keywords in addition to your potential business name just to be sure (for example, keywords relating to where you will be doing business or who your audience is).

- ✧ **State Sites:** If you're in the US, the first place you should check is your state's business registry website. In some states, the name search is part of the registration process, but not in all of them.

- ✧ **Trademark Database:** Head to www.uspto.gov/trademarks/search to search for your name and similar names.

YOUR AESTHETIC

The visual aesthetic of your brand includes your logo, color palette, and typography. These are all parts of your brand's identity that should not only match what you have already been building but can also enhance it. If you want your brand to be unique enough to attract your dream audience and turn them into customers, you will need to create a look that will stand out and make sure it is cohesive across all of your platforms.

When developing your brand's aesthetic, you'll want to keep in mind that even though you will be communicating with your prospects and customers through your brand's tone or personality (see next step), there is quite a bit of psychology to the visual aspects as well. There are certain colors and fonts that make people feel a certain way. Also, remember that when people visit your website or social media pages for the first time, they may not remember everything that the page says, but they will remember how it made them feel.

YOUR COLOR PALETTE

Your color palette is made up of two to four different colors that you will use across all of your marketing materials, including your logo and anywhere else your brand is represented. A study done by Color Communications Innovations' Institute for Color Research found that people make a subconscious judgment about a person, environment, or product within ninety seconds of their initial viewing. Between 62 percent and 90 percent of that initial assessment is based on color alone. According to a study by the University of Loyola, Maryland, color increases brand recognition up to 80 percent.

Jefa in Training

Aside from associating feelings with colors, there have also been studies done regarding what colors are attractive to people of different genders and various cultural backgrounds. Depending on who your audience is, you may want to do more research, but here is a basic breakdown of traits associated with the most popular colors.

Red: Symbolizes energy, excitement, and passion. Often used to draw attention, create urgency, or encourage.

Blue: Symbolizes calm, trust, and responsibility. Often used to reduce stress or ensure security.

Green: Symbolizes growth, tranquility, and freshness. Often used to promote benefits, abundance, and wellness.

Purple: Symbolizes romance, luxury, and mystery. Often used to enhance creativity, intuition, and strength.

Yellow: Symbolizes happiness and friendship. Often used to heighten awareness and foster analytical thinking.

For example, if you want your brand to convey a feeling of leisure, consider choosing colors that represent the ocean waves, palm trees, and a sandy beach—like tan, blue, and green tones. If you want to be bold and express strength, you can use colors like red and purple.

YOUR TYPOGRAPHY

Just as color can call forth feelings from someone just learning about your brand for the first time, typography can do the same. To establish brand recognition, you will want to do the same as with colors and go with only a couple of fonts.

Fonts evoke an atmosphere associated with their design. Sans serif fonts, for example, are seen as modern and versatile. Verdana is light and thin and is often considered elegant. Handwritten fonts are more artistic and informal. You can also use a mix of all of these to express different things in your marketing. The main things you'll want to make sure of when choosing fonts for your business messaging is that they should work on all platforms, that they are (of course) legible, and that they can be bolded, italicized, and so on when used in different contexts.

YOUR LOGO

Your logo will be a combination of your color palette, your chosen typography, and any kind of symbols you think best represent your brand. A good logo will work at any size and can be used in any format—print, online, or on merchandise. Your logo should be unique, memorable, attractive to your target audience, and timeless.

Para Más Inspiración: Un Consejo
An Exercise to Help You Visualize from Vanessa Castillo

"Focus on who you are as a brand, not what you do as a brand."

—Vanessa Castillo

Entrepreneur and branding coach Vanessa Castillo, who has helped Miami's top creatives and influencers solidify their image, encourages her clients to create mood boards on Pinterest. You can also do this by saving Google Images you like in a folder or even simply cutting things out of magazines—it's up to you!

To start, all you need is to create a collage of photos that you like. You can do this for all of the different parts of building your brand. Once you create your first collage, notice any trends in the aesthetic of the photos that you chose and start to build your color palette based on what you see. Do you notice a certain style being represented in your collage? Is it modern in look, or perhaps more classic? What do you see?

YOUR VOICE

Last but certainly not least, you will want to think about the tone you'll be using to connect with your audience. When your brand speaks, what is its personality? Do you want to be funny, approachable, sarcastic, or something else entirely? What kind of language will you use in your marketing—will you use slang or keep it professional? Think about how you want your audience to feel: empowered, ambitious, joyful, or serious?

Look at some of the brands that you follow and take note of how they engage their community. Notice what you like and what you dislike about their tone.

Putting It All Together

Taken together, the aesthetic components and the voice you choose make up the baseline of your brand's style. It's a good idea to put together a style guide that collects all of the specifics for your brand in one central document. This will make it easier if you choose to work with a designer; and down the line, it will be something helpful to send to collaborators.

YOUR STYLE GUIDE CHECKLIST

- ☐ Tone and messaging guidelines (e.g., approachable, inclusive, evokes empowerment, etc.)

- ☐ Typography standards (fonts to avoid, when to use bold or italicize, etc.)

- ☐ How to use the logo (including sizing and variations in color and style)

  - If you have different logos for different uses, you can include them here. For example, if you have an image with text and a design, perhaps you'll want to create three different versions of it to use where you see fit: one with just text, one with just the design, and one with both combined.

- ☐ Color palette—Include three to four main colors and two secondary colors just in case.

- ☐ Different ways to use branding in print versus online:

  - Aside from different logo sizing and variations in style as mentioned above, you'll also want to make sure all text is readable (check your fonts and colors) and that arrangements of any images are suitable for any scenario. Especially when looking at digital assets, ensure that all designs will also look clean on mobile devices.

- ☐ Editorial style guidelines—Do you have a preference between MLA, Chicago, or AP Style?

From visuals to messaging, there are many parts to building your brand, and this chapter's ejercicio includes a Branding Cheat Sheet for you to fill out. But first, here are some key takeaways from the chapter.

Key Takeaways from Lección 3

- Your brand will encompass many aspects, including the colors and type with which you represent yourself, the tone you use when communicating with your followers, the partners with whom you align yourself, and the ideas that you stand behind.

- Setting brand values that are in line with your vision and mission will help you genuinely connect with your audience down the line. Think about what is important to you; this may turn out to be what separates you from everyone else.

- Establishing a consistent aesthetic with colors, type, and logos is just as important as your voice—give thought to how you visually communicate with your community.

¡Manos a La Obra!

A Branding Cheat Sheet in collaboration with Vanessa Castillo of VCV Agency

About Your Business

What is your brand's mission?

_____

_____

What is your brand vision?

_____

_____

What are your brand values?

_____

_____

About Your Target Audience

Who do you serve? Age, location, income, etc.

_____

_____

Brand Aesthetics

Which specific colors do you like for your brand?

_____

What style of typography or fonts do you like? (Select one to three fonts)

_____

What logo elements are you typically drawn to?

_____

Brand Voice

How do you want people to feel when they read your messaging on your site, social media, and/or ads?

_____

List a few words to include in your style guide about the *tone* you will use when communicating on behalf of your business.

_____

_____

_____

Now go and create, ¡jefas! Buena suerte.

"Me gustan las personas que tienen que luchar para obtener algo. Los que, teniéndolo todo en contra, salen adelante."

-Isabel Allende

Lección 4

Prepárate

You have now built a solid foundation for your brand with your mission, vision, and values, and you have the tools to start moving it forward. But before you do, there are a few more things that you need to make sure are solid not only to protect your ideas, services, and products, but to set yourself up for sustainable growth legally and financially.

Launching a project is always exciting, and for first timers, it is easy to overlook these steps. For most of us, reading up on LLCs, nonprofits, contracts, and budgets is the not-so-fun part of the creation process. Nonetheless, it is extremely important, and this chapter will guide you through legal and financial matters while providing the resources you need to make the process easier.

*Disclosure: I am not an attorney or an accountant, therefore any information in this chapter is based on knowledge I have gathered from successful Latinas who are in fact licensed to do this work. I am always going to point you in the best direction I can, but for legal and financial matters, I do recommend that you hire a professional.

Protecting Your Business

In this section, we are going to dive into the legal status of your business. Its legal status will not only affect how you can accept and track money, but also how you pay taxes.

If you did not already do so in the last chapter, complete a comprehensive search of your brand name. Remember that you will want something that is unique to you and has staying power. This name will be attached to your business website, social media, email address, logo, ads, public relations, and more—so the further you go with your business, the more rebranding will be a lengthy and pricey process. Do not take this decision lightly! If you try to register a business with a name that is already registered and trademarked, the name will not be approved—and using a name that belongs to someone else can expose you to legal problems in the future. Refer to the sidebar in Lección 3 to cross-reference all the important sources. If you do not have the time to do this yourself, a lawyer who specializes in intellectual property and trademark law can do a search for a fee.

Select a Business Entity y Regístrate!

While you can find the differences between the various kinds of business entities with a simple Google search, I have included them here for quick reference. There are a few more out there that I will not include as they will not pertain to most of you, but as you grow further into your business, note that while you can change your business entity later, it will cost you financially. I've broken down the main types of business entities below:

Sole Proprietorship

If you have already been monetizing a side hustle, you are probably familiar with sole proprietorships. In some states, you do not even have to register for this kind of entity and you are automatically considered a sole proprietorship if you are doing business activities but have not registered your business. Keep in mind, this means that there is no legal separation between you and your business, meaning you can be held personally responsible for its debts. Since most banks are hesitant to lend to sole proprietorships, raising money can be challenging.

To summarize: Licensing your business as a sole proprietorship is recommended if you're trying out a low-risk business idea, but it's not recommended if you plan on trying to get investors or taking out a loan.

LLC

Registering as an LLC protects you by separating your personal and business assets. This means that if your business faces bankruptcy or lawsuits, your personal assets will not be affected. There are certain tax benefits to registering as an LLC as well, like writing off acceptable expenses (which we will talk more about in another section).

In sum: Recommended for medium- to high-risk business ideas that you are hoping to scale.

Nonprofit Corporation

Nonprofits, also known as charities and foundations, are mission-driven organizations that are established to do social good. If you want to

set up a nonprofit, you not only have to register with your state, but if you want to have tax-exempt status (meaning you will not have to pay federal taxes on any profits made), you will have to file a separate application with the IRS (IRS Form 1023). Keep in mind that much like larger corporations, nonprofits must follow strict rules on how they spend the money they make and must file annual reports with the IRS.

Para Más Inspiración: Un Tip

If you're thinking about going the nonprofit route, look into acquiring a fiscal sponsor. Fiscal sponsorship allows you to use the tax exemption status of your sponsor for donations and grants, and some sponsors even provide coaching. There are certain organizations that take on outside projects as affiliates. In return, they take a percentage of the tax-deductible income your organization brings in, though you will still have to pay taxes on the earned income.

Register for Your Business License

Every state in the USA has different requirements as far as how to register and maintain your business status. You can find this on your state's website, where it is sometimes called the Division of Corporations. (To look up the department where you can register your business in your state, check the Small Business Administration's website at: https://www.sba.gov/business-guide/launch-your-business/register-your-business.) The business registration process generally includes these steps:

1. Register on your state's website and pay the business license fee, which in some states must be renewed yearly.

2. Obtain an Employer Identification Number (EIN) if you are not a sole proprietorship; this is free through the IRS website.

3. Secure any additional documentation, like operating agreements and bylaws.

Para Más Inspiración: Unos Consejos

The Top Five Legal Mistakes Entrepreneurs Make When Launching Their Business from Jacqueline Garcia-Arteaga

There are many things to take into consideration when choosing your business entity. IP Guru founder Jacqueline Garcia-Arteaga is a Miami-based licensed intellectual property lawyer who helps Latina creatives secure their independence by legally protecting their businesses and brands. She believes the single most important thing for new entrepreneurs to think about when choosing a business entity is liability.

> "Think of legal advice the same way [you] view getting medical attention. It is best when it is preventative rather than curative—a preliminary search on your name may cost you sixty dollars, versus a trademark infringement, which can cost thousands."
>
> —Jacqueline Garcia-Arteaga

DIY Google Search Versus Attorney Consultation

A business and trademark attorney will know exactly what you need to legally protect yourself and your business. While a Google search may give you some information, every business is different, and therefore each one's legal needs are different too.

Failure to Conduct a Prelaunch Search Before Purchasing Domains or Other Registrations

A business should always conduct a preliminary search on their brand name before moving forward with any purchases or publications. Without meaning to, a business owner may be violating someone's trademark rights, which could result in them owing the trademark owner monetary compensation.

Copyright Is Not the Same as Trademarked

Before a brand launches, the owner of the brand should meet with a trademark attorney. When you have a trademark on your brand, you have the legal right to exclusive use of your brand identifier, including the name, logo, and any associated brand slogan in the category of goods or services you plan to provide. A copyright is a right to publish original material. As a business owner, it is necessary to have a clear idea of how the two are different. Trademarks identify the source of a good or service. Copyrights protect intellectual expressions contained in books, audio and video recordings, performances, and so on. The two are very different. As discussed above, launching a business under a brand name without first checking to make sure the name has not previously been registered can result in trademark infringement.

Failure to Legally Secure Your LLC or Corporation

Every state has their own requirements for what you must do to establish and maintain an LLC or corporation; any competent local business lawyer will be up on what is required. The most frequent mistake is not writing up a contract between the business owner and the business detailing how the business will be run and maintained. If you have an LLC, this is called an operating agreement; if you have a corporation, it's called the bylaws. These documents should be regularly updated and

reviewed. Know and uphold the legal requirements, like paying annual fees and avoiding commingling of personal and business assets—or take the risk of your business losing its liability protection.

Lack of Specific Contracts

In a contract, it is crucial to outline in detail exactly what the contract is about, including exactly how the service will be performed or the goods will be delivered, exactly how and when you expect to get paid, and so on. When you use premade templates that you find online, it is impossible to know whether that contract is truly protecting you in the ways you need, since every business is different. Working with an attorney is highly recommended to spot areas where you may need protection and ensure your rights are safeguarded in your business contracts.

Why Is Selecting the Correct Business Entity Important?

Aside from liability protection, the type of business entity you choose will also affect how you pay taxes. Unless you are a tax-exempt organization, you will have to pay taxes based on different state and federal laws. According to Vanessa Duran, a certified tax professional, one of the top mistakes entrepreneurs make when it comes to taxes is not having the correct tax structure for their business—one that serves both their personal and business goals.

As a new entrepreneur, you may have questions about how taxes work, how much to save, and so on—and that is exactly what we're about to cover.

As you read this section, keep in mind that this is just general advice to help give you some background to be better informed if and when you choose to work with a tax professional.

~~~~~~

Para Más Inspiración: Unos Consejos

¿Que Onda Con Taxes? from Vanessa Duran

Vanessa Duran is a Colombian-born tax accountant based in Miami who is the founder of DCC Accounting, a financial accounting and management consulting firm for small businesses. She sat down with me to provide an introduction to taxes for the new business owner, along with some tips on how to best ensure that you set the financial foundation of your business up for success.

When Should We File Taxes?

Business income tax returns are filed once a year; however, you may be required to pay estimated tax, which is paid quarterly. Anyone with an expected tax liability of a thousand dollars or more should pay quarterly estimated tax. If you anticipate making a profit, consult your tax advisor to determine how much your expected tax liability will be based on your expected business income. This will help you determine your quarterly tax.

How Much Do We Need to Save for Taxes?

How much you need to set aside will depend on a few things. The first step is to find out what your marginal tax rate is prior to going into business; begin this process by finding out applicable tax rates where you are. Understanding how your local tax brackets work is particularly important if you will be filing taxes jointly with your spouse. If this is what you normally do, you should know that if you have a single member

LLC or a sole proprietorship, you can file your business tax as part of your personal taxes. If you don't file taxes separately from your spouse and your business is your only source of income, your business income will be taxed at a higher marginal tax rate (unless your business is a C-corporation that pays taxes to a separate entity).

After you have figured out the marginal tax rate that applies to your business, estimate your business's net income for the year and multiply that number by the tax rate to figure out your potential annual business tax. (Example: Your marginal tax rate multiplied by your potential business income = income tax savings.) If your business is classified as a partnership or a sole proprietorship, you will need to add in self-employment tax, which is an extra 15.3 percent tax on your self-employment income.

In addition, there are a few more tax rates that you should be aware of as you grow:

- ✦ Corporate tax rates in the state where you incorporate or license your business.
- ✦ If you hire employees, you'll have to pay employment taxes.
- ✦ If sales tax must legally be paid by those who buy your product, you'll have to file sales tax returns and register to pay them in the states where you're selling.

As mentioned previously, this is just an introduction to what taxes can involve, keeping in mind that everyone's situation can be different. There is a lot to consider when filing taxes for your business, but working with a tax professional rather than a tax software like TurboTax has its benefits. By working with a professional, you will get more personalized experience. It's an initial investment, but if they're able to help you maximize deductions and make sure your records are in order, it could save you more money than it costs in the long run.

Key Takeaways from Lección 4

▶ Legal advice is best when it is preventative rather than curative. Get help before anything unfortunate happens.

▶ Do a comprehensive name search before registering anything.

▶ Choosing the wrong business entity type could affect your personal financial liability.

▶ Do not wait until tax time to do your books and only find out then how much money you have made or not made. Calculate how much you have to save for taxes and put it away ahead of time.

¡Manos a La Obra!

Your Legal Checklist

- ❑ Did you conduct a preliminary search on your name to make certain it is free of trademark infringement?

- ❑ Did you choose which type of business entity will be best for your venture?

    - • Circle which one:
      LLC, Sole Proprietorship, Nonprofit, other?

- ❑ Did you register your business with your state?

    - • How much was your registration fee?_____

    - • When does it expire? _____

- ❑ Did you secure an EIN (Employer Identification Number)?

    - • Write it here: _____

- ❑ Do you have an operating agreement or bylaws in place?

- ❑ What percentage of your business's income will you put away for taxes? _____

- ❑ When will you pay your taxes?

    - • Write in when you will file taxes for this year _____

"El dinero llama al dinero."

Lección 5

El Dinero Habla

Money talks—and getting comfortable with finances will be what makes or breaks your business. You can have great ideas, but if you really want to turn those ideas into something sustainable, you have to manage your cash flow. According to SCORE.org, as of 2020, 82 percent of small businesses fail because of cash flow issues—but have no fear, this chapter will prepare you so that you can stay on top of what comes in and goes out of your business bank account.

In the last chapter, we went over how important it is to account for the correct amount of taxes you'll have to pay as a business owner; however, that is only part of what you'll need to take into consideration when you are building out your financial plan. In the next few pages, you're going to create a plan to set yourself up for financial success when you are starting out: what to consider when you are figuring out your pricing, how to check in with your finances throughout the process, and how to diversify your revenue streams so that you can have a sustainable business for years to come.

This chapter will first provide you with some basics on what's important to consider in terms of finances while building your business and will then guide you in the creation of your very own one-page financial plan (aka your OFP). This OFP will include a proposed budget, an actual budget and metrics tracker all in one, and a modified version of the spreadsheet template created by Vanessa Duran (founder of DCC

Accounting). It will be a tool you use to calculate the break-even point and growth potential of your business.

Familiarizing Yourself with Finances

Getting Started

Starting any new venture requires you to take a look at not only your business goals but your personal goals as well. Ask yourself these two questions: Will this venture be able to fund the lifestyle you need? Beyond that—does it have the potential to provide you with the lifestyle you want for your future? If you're unsure, that's okay. Part of the reason you will create this plan is to help you figure out how and when you'll realistically be able to reach those goals.

To create this plan, start with a base number—your required monthly income. What is the amount you need to sustain yourself as you get your business off the ground? It's up to you whether or not to keep your outside full-time job or work a part-time day job to make ends meet while you launch and work toward profitability, but whatever that number is, it will be key to the future success of the business.

Remember, it is important to be able to grow your business at a pace that works for you—sometimes that might mean it takes a few years to become profitable, and because of that, it's essential to know the minimum you that can live off. You should not have to worry about how you will pay your rent, buy food, and so on, but if you're going all in, it might mean that you will have to work toward being able to pay yourself an amount that allows for more "wants" versus just covering your needs.

Before we can create a projection based on how much you will sell, you will not only need to know what you are selling but also have a good idea of pricing. To determine pricing, you'll want to consider these three things:

THE COST

Depending on what kind of business you are launching, you'll have a variety of costs that you'll need to cover to get started, but some will also be recurring expenses you incur to make products, ship items, market your business, and more.

Here is a list of the most common business expenses—check them off if they apply to you:

❑ Costs and legal fees for business license, copyright, and/or trademark

$ _____

❑ Domain registration costs

$ _____

❑ Website hosting monthly/yearly fees

$ _____

❑ Newsletter platform costs

$ _____

❑ Client management monthly/yearly costs

$ _____

- ❏ Accounting software (if you feel you need it)

  $ _____

- ❏ Materials to make your products

  $ _____

  - ❏ If you're importing, remember to check tariffs!

    $ _____

- ❏ Packaging materials

  $ _____

- ❏ Brand design costs (logo, other materials you might need like for a photoshoot for social media content, creating a brand guide, etc.)

  $ _____

- ❏ Shipping costs

  $ _____

Other costs you will want to consider:

- ❏ Marketing costs: This includes everything from design software (Canva or Photoshop) or hiring graphic designers to a social media scheduler or a social media manager, ads, etc.

  $ _____

- ❏ Networking costs: LinkedIn Premium and other membership communities

  $ _____

- ❏ Travel costs: Do you need to see clients in person? Seek out vendors to work with?

  $ _____

Do you have any other costs for your business? Add them here:

_____

_____

_____

Based on the total amount you'll be investing up front and the estimated monthly recurring costs of your business, how much will you need to cover your business expenses in your first year?

$ _____

YOUR CAPACITY

Knowing your capacity is also important to build your financial plan, and it's a skill you'll need in order to scale your business as well. Not only will you need to plan for the resources needed to build your business, you'll also need to consider time spent on marketing, selling, packaging, and actually creating your products and/or meeting with your clients.

How many hours can you dedicate to your business each week? How many of those hours will be directly associated with making money? Do you have the resources (space, staff, or money up front for materials) required to create X amount of products? If you don't have the resources or the time, do you need to outsource in order to hit your financial goals? Those outsourcing costs will have to be added to your expenses.

(MONEY-SPECIFIC) MARKET RESEARCH

Once you figure out what your capacity and expenses are, you need to come up with a sample price for your product. You can validate your chosen price points by asking your target audience for feedback and researching what your competitors are charging.

You'll also want to get familiar with the size of your potential market is and the scope of their buying power. Can they afford to buy your services and/or products? How often? Will you rely on the same people making repeat purchases to reach your goals? Or will you have to attract new buyers every month?

Your pricing will of course also depend on your capacity, experience, and a variety of other factors depending on your industry.

Setting Your Pricing

Taking into consideration your costs, capacity, and potential customer base, it's time to set your pricing.

Here's an example of how a service-based business might develop their pricing.

Cindy is starting her business as a life coach while still working full-time as a teacher. She currently only has ten hours each week to take on new clients, but down the line, she'd love to be able to scale her business and coach full-time. To start, she'd like to be able to make at least two thousand dollars a month from her business. If she is able to take on forty client session hours per month and we divide that number of hours by two thousand dollars, that would be fifty dollars an hour.

However, that number doesn't account for her taxes and expenses. Cindy is a life coach, so her overhead is minimal. It consists of a $15 monthly website fee and a client management software subscription payment of $20. Her estimated taxes based on state tax rates and her income bracket are about 25 percent.

At the specified rates, taxes on $2,000 would be about $500, with an additional $35 in monthly expenses. That's an extra $535 a month that Cindy needs to add into her pricing if she wants to take home $2,000 a month. So in reality, she needs to charge at least $63 per hour in order to hit her goal.

Her formula is:

**(Her Goal Number + Taxes + Expenses)
divided by her Total Hours Worked**

For product-based businesses, you'll need to look at how much time it takes you to make your products and how many you're able to make on your own in a given amount of time.

With all being said, there is no a one-size-fits-all formula for working out pricing. Your pricing may also depend the following:

▶ Demand, meaning you might increase pricing during the busy season.

▶ Market share, meaning you're lowering your pricing to get more customers and build loyalty as opposed to making more money immediately.

In any case, you'll want to add some cushion to your prices so that you can offer special discounts that won't put you in the negative when you're analyzing your budget at the end of the month.

Setting and Tracking Financial Goals

To start, you're going to build your first projected budget based not only on your capacity to create and execute, but also on how much you can sell. Think about the size of your network and how many potential customers you know. Do you already have a newsletter or social media accounts you've been building? Are you part of online networks where you could make sales? You can even do a "soft launch" to your family, friends, and acquaintances to test the market.

Here's one example of how a pool of new customers can be developed: Businesses can offer free pockets of time to do "clarity" calls and then give discounts to certain groups for say three months, following up by evaluating how those efforts tied into to new sales.

To see how this might play out, let's take Cindy from the pricing exercise. If she announces free twenty-five-minute clarity calls on social media and books ten people for calls, those are ten leads! After her post-call follow-ups, let's say she gains four ongoing clients. The next month, she does the same and gets similar results. For Cindy, that might mean that on average for every ten leads, she'll get four clients—at that rate, she can estimate how many new potential clients she'll need to speak with every month.

En suma, you'll want to conduct market research to validate pricing, calculate the size of your potential market to figure out demand, and consider the quantity you can put out in order to determine your capacity.

Once You've Launched

It is recommended that you update your budget quarterly, but to better keep a finger on the pulse of your business, you can do a Budget vs. Actual Analysis. For your first month, this would be more of a *forecasted* vs. actual analysis, but it will help you identify any extra spending and what products or services aren't selling, determine if you need to increase your pricing, and more.

For your Budget vs. Actual Analysis, you will be comparing the original budget you created (in which you projected how much you would need to spend on your business each month) to your actual monthly expenses and income to date. If doing the analysis shows you that the numbers differ, you then have the opportunity to make changes to generate better outcomes the next month.

For example, if you're incurring expenses going to a lot of networking events, it's possible that you might overspend one month, and you'll want to make sure that doesn't become a consistent pattern. If it *does* turn out to be a necessary expense in your budget, you can plan to cover that expense the next month by increasing your sales goals.

Diversifying Your Revenue Streams

If it's hard to imagine selling enough of your service or product to cover the costs of running your business, it might be time to think about diversifying your revenue streams. Multiple revenue streams are great to generate extra income but can also save you in case something goes south and you for some reason cannot offer one or two of your services or products.

For service-based businesses, diversifying revenue streams might mean offering products like a subscription community with courses and templates, or it could mean hosting master classes and doing speaking engagements. For product-based businesses, it could also mean hosting events as well as cocreating products with partners. It could also mean adding on items that are of low additional cost to you but of high value to them. For example, if you own a candle making company, perhaps it's a DIY candle making kit, or if you're an online clothing boutique, maybe a curated quarterly box.

The key to developing additional profitable revenue streams is to look at your current customer base (or your ideal base if you have not yet launched). What else could they be interested in? What else do they need that is not far from what you already offer and doesn't have a large startup cost?

Take note of the questions your audience may already be asking you. If you have heard "Do you offer _____?" or "I would buy it if you included _____" more than a handful of times, it is something to consider.

Key Takeaways from Lección 5

- ❋ Know how much money you need to bring in per month to be able to run your business and pay yourself.

- ❋ You will set your pricing based on your costs, capacity, and the buying potential of your customer base.

- ❋ It is recommended that you update your budget every quarter, but to have a better read on the financial health of your business, you can do a Budget vs. Actual Analysis to help identify any unexpected spending, what products or services aren't selling, whether you need to increase your prices, and more.

- ❋ Be open to expanding what your business offers to diversify your revenue streams.

- ❋ Keep clean records; use a spreadsheet at first if needed.

- ❋ Remember that you are not alone and that there are professionals out there to support you!

¡Manos a La Obra!

Creating Your One-Page Financial Plan

The One-Page Financial Plan (OFP) is a budget and financial goals tracker spreadsheet developed by Vanessa Duran, founder of DCC Accounting. Here is a model form to help you create a spreadsheet of your own by filling out the fields on the next page.

Start by figuring out your personal budget, including your total monthly personal expenses. That figure will determine how much you need to make when you pay yourself from your business.

Once you decide on that number, move on to figuring out your projected business revenue, which is calculated by taking the prices of the different services or products (i.e., revenue sources) you plan to offer and estimating how many of each of them you think you'll sell each month, then multiplying each price by that quantity.

You'll also take note of your business expenses on this chart—if you're a solopreneur, your business revenue minus your expenses and taxes should leave you with the amount you need to pay yourself.

With that goal in mind, use the Strategy section to note what needs to happen for you to hit these goals, the KPI section to write in actionable steps, and the Goal for Month section to write in exact numbers reflecting your aim. As the months go by and you reflect on what has worked and what hasn't, make ongoing entries in the Learn, Track, and New Experiments sections.

At the bottom, you can also evaluate how many hours you've worked, how much profit and net income you've made per offering, and if your potential monthly income is up to what you're aiming for based on your capacity. Revisit this OFP monthly and make edits as needed. Buena suerte!

Personal Budget	Monthly Payment	Strategy	KPI = Key Performance Indicators	Learn
Total Monthly Expenses	$	(Example: Launch new products or services)	(Example: Send email or direct messages to over 100 people this month)	(How did your Key Performance Indicators affect your goal? How close to it did you get?)
Business Revenue				
Revenue Source 1				
Revenue Source 2				
Total	$			
Business Expenses		**Goal for Month**	**Track**	**New Experiments**
Materials		(Sell X amount of products or services)	(Did you meet the goals for the month?)	(What will you try next month to get you closer to your goals?)
Software				
Misc.				
Total	$			
Hours Worked Monthly				
Income Per Unit	$			
Potential Monthly Income	$			

"Yo no me mido por las expectativas de los demás o dejo que otros definan mi valor."

-Sonia Sotomayor

Lección 6

Ser Diferente Es Ser Fuerte

When people first have an idea for a project and someone asks, "Why don't you start this as a serious venture?" the usual responses are, "Well, there are already so many out there like this" or "A million people do this already."

While that all might be true, what is also true is that no one else is you. No one grew up exactly the way you did, no one had to overcome the exact obstacles that you have, no one has had the exact experiences you have—and no one communicates, does business, or creates content exactly the way you do.

You have a unique perspective; therefore, you will create a unique business and product. It can be intimidating to see everything else that is out there, and you may even experience a bit of imposter syndrome, but you do deserve a seat at this table—the entrepreneur table, la mesa de las jefas.

No matter how different you think you are—perhaps because you are not doing business in your native language, didn't go to college, or started out with a career in a completely different field—you have strengths that are going to guide you through this process *and* help you stand out and build reputation in your industry. Those strengths plus the values embodied in your business will make up the core of your Unique Selling Proposition.

How to Stand Out in Your Industry

Identifying Your Unique Selling Proposition

Your Unique Selling Proposition (USP, also known as unique value proposition) is essentially your unique perspective. It will play a huge part in your marketing strategy, both as you launch and as your business grows.

The key to identifying your USP is to analyze who you are and where you stand in the market. Doing some market research is a great place to start, but here is where you can get even more detailed: note what your competitors do and how they do it versus what you do and how you do it differently.

Why Identifying Your USP Is Important

I once worked with a four-year-old tech startup whose main competitor had been around for twenty years. They had similar features and in fact, in a lot of ways, the older company offered more in-depth features. Yet their longtime customers (who had entered into multiple year contracts) were moving over to this younger startup. Not only were they switching companies, but they were also telling their friends.

While the younger startup had a small team and limited resources, they took a good look early on at what their competitors were doing—not just when they started but as they continued to grow. The startup had many unique selling points that differentiated them from these other well-known companies. The other companies hadn't made their services easy or affordable; this startup was out to change the landscape by filling those needs.

HERE'S WHAT THEY MANAGED TO DO DIFFERENTLY

THEY BUILT A FLEXIBLE FINANCIAL MODEL BASED ON THEIR CLIENTS' GROWTH

While a risky model for a startup, compared to their competitors, they had a very minimal onboarding fee, they took a lower percentage of the proceeds of their clients' sales, and they lacked any requirement to commit to long-term binding contracts. These qualities appealed to their target audience and proved that the company was invested in their clients' success—who doesn't want a tech partner like that?

FEATURES WERE PUSHED OUT FAST AND THEY KEPT THEM 100 PERCENT BASED ON COMMUNITY NEEDS

In the space of technology business, especially with larger companies, it can sometimes take years to push out new features, take them through testing and beta stages, and then officially launch them. This startup worked around the clock not only to keep up with industry standards in a changing world (i.e., during COVID-19) but also to incorporate client requests like features, bug fixes, and updates within twenty-four hours.

CUSTOMER SUPPORT WAS THEIR PRIORITY

Not only did this startup make sure they were approachable to new clients, they also made sure they were responsive to current ones. They set out to hire client success specialists with diverse backgrounds who were familiar with the pain points of their target audience. That way, their team could come up with solutions and provide product feedback before clients even saw the products.

Since they were a startup, this company did not have to go through as many hoops as large corporations. Features were based not only on the current needs of the client base, but future needs as well. Clients were excited to work with a startup that took their feedback seriously enough to implement changes.

Along with competitive pricing, great customer experience, and innovative features, the startup held live product demos. Here, consumers met with startup founders to ask them about current and future features. The founders of this startup were personable and passionate about serving the needs of their clients—and you could tell that just by speaking to them. These live demos converted between 65 percent and 70 percent of demo attendees into loyal clients.

Other Ways to Stand Out

Using Your Personal Strengths

If you have strong communication skills and easily connect with people, that's part of your USP. Let people learn a little more about you! If you are providing a service, consider hosting webinars or making short "intro" calls. Give them a glimpse of what it's like to work with you or use your products; show them who you are and share your "why" with potential clients.

Create a Business Model That Aligns with Your Values

If you are creating a mission-driven brand, one way to stand out is to give back! Volunteer some of your skills, give products to charity, discount offerings to nonprofit leaders, or if you can, donate to organizations you are passionate about. People will feel better knowing they are giving to a business that gives back, especially if they perceive your company's efforts as sincere.

Make It Easy to Work with You

Answering messages in a timely manner, giving every one of your clients personalized attention, and forming genuine relationships with them—*that* creates a unique experience. When people repurchase from you or refer others, it's because they felt supported. Just as the previous example demonstrated, people will remember their experience and how you made them feel. That goes a long way! You will see this come up in the reviews people leave, the number of direct referrals you get, and the customers that return.

How to Clearly and Effectively Summarize Your USP

Now that you have a short list that sums up what you bring to the table, think about how you can use these strengths and opportunities to bring your ideal customer to you. Your pitch will be a couple of sentences that combines what your ideal customer wants and what your business does well. This will be what's on your website and in your client pitches, and of course it should all fit in your Instagram bio at no more than 150 characters.

Para Más Inspiración: Un Ejemplo

Pitches Que Inspiran

Here are a couple of examples from inspiring Latina founders:

- ✧ Ceremonia, founded by Babba C. Rivera—her pitch is short and effective: Clean Haircare rooted in Latinx Heritage.
- ✧ Rizos Curls by Julissa Prado: Curls, Community, Culture—con mucho amor.

Test Your Offerings

If you are stuck on finding the best words to describe you or your business, this is where you can call in some help. Identify some friends and family that are interested in what you plan to offer, give them a sample, and gather some testimonials.

Once people have been introduced to your product or service, take some of the most common adjectives they use to describe it and see if you can incorporate their impressions into your pitch.

For example, if you are a coach, you may want to share your clients' results. Do you help your clients identify their blind spots? Strengthen the foundations of their new businesses to help them grow efficiently? Do they describe you as empathetic, or as strategic? These are all great to include when aiming to prove that you do things differently and better.

Using Your USP to Your Advantage

Just as with the startup I described earlier , it is important to know where you stand in your industry and to consistently represent that everywhere—on your website and social media, as well as in demos, ads, and whatever other channels you use to reach new clients.

Here are some ideas to get you started:

▶ **Show Your Impact:** Incorporate statistics into your website. Show how your business is directly impacting your clients. What have your clients been able to do since they started working with you or buying your product?

▶ **Leave Them Inspired:** When people are first starting to get to know your brand, it's important to share your "why." What are your core values? What do you hope to change in your industry? What gap did you see in your market that you wanted to fill? What made you start it all?

▶ **Share Your Journey:** Are you in the midst of planning a new product launch? Are you expanding to a new location? Did you just get funding to grow? People like to feel like they are investing in something that is putting their money toward growth, so do not be afraid to share the different stages of your business.

▶ **Be Authentically You y Cuenta Tu Historia!:** Remember that what makes you diferente is what makes you fuerte. Especially as a solopreneur, you want people to connect with you—and you can do that by telling your story and humanizing your brand. Some of the most successful ad campaigns are based on these kinds of stories. The more people feel connected with you, the more they will buy into your brand.

Key Takeaways from Lección 6

* The key to identifying your Unique Selling Proposition is to first analyze who you are and where you stand in the market.

* Be aware of who your competitors are, what they do well, and what they could do better—this is where you can shine and make a name for yourself.

* Using your personal strengths, aligning your brand with your values, and being easy to work with can help move you forward.

* Make sure your USP is written concisely—use keywords that will grab people's attention.

* Back it up by sharing your journey and telling your story through your social media platforms, your website—everywhere!

¡Manos a La Obra!

Defining Your Unique Selling Proposition

For this exercise, we're going to break it into two parts!

In Chapter One, we covered how to conduct a competitive analysis as well as how to do a SWOT analysis—in this first part of the exercise, we're going to merge these two strategies to help inspire you as you develop your USP. In the chart below, list five of your competitors: In the first column, write the name of the competitor; in the second column, list three to five things you think they are doing well; and in the third, three to five things you think they could be doing better.

Once you've done this, list an equal number of strengths you have that can help you meet needs that aren't currently being met. This will help you see the opportunities to bring something different into the market.

The next step is to turn those strengths—your experience, skills, and so on—into a pitch that you can share with the world. We're going to practice the infamous elevator pitch. Think about what you would say to someone if you only had thirty seconds to tell them about who you are and what you do, get them interested enough to have a longer conversation with you, and secure them as a customer.

Competitor	Competitor Strengths	Competitor Weaknesses	Your Strengths

Remember, this can incorporate what you think makes you diferente—your team, how you develop products, and so on. What need do you see in your industry, and how can you uniquely fill it?

To get started, fill out the following formula:

What You Offer + Who Your Customers Are + How You Do It Differently = Your Pitch

Por ejemplo:

Brand X offers technology to help nonprofits fundraise at their in-person, hybrid, and virtual events. We're not just a technology partner—we're an extension of your team, and we don't believe in locking you into contracts.

_____

_____

_____

_____

_____

_____

Now that you have your pitch—let's use it. A lo que sigue, jefas!

"Si te cierran una puerta, cuélate por una ventana."

-Luz Maria Doria

Lección 7

A Vender

Idea, check!
Legal, check!
Unique Selling Proposition, check!

Selling is by definition the process of exchanging money for goods and services. For business owners, the term "sales" is used to describe the different ways you *lead* people to buy into what you have to offer.

This chapter will help you understand how sales and marketing work together, as well as how to build a sales strategy, generate leads, and convert those leads into fully engaged and loyal customers.

Sales Estrategias 101

What Is a Sales Strategy?

Building a sales strategy is an essential part of a plan for long-term revenue growth through attracting new customers (aka *acquisition*) while holding onto existing customers (aka *retention*).

Sales and marketing go hand in hand. Marketing, which the next chapter will cover, is the process of building awareness of your brand. Sales is the process of turning that awareness into dollars. The sales process starts with the people you attract through marketing and PR, who in marketing are called "leads." Your inbound leads come from your organic content, such as blog posts, search engine optimization (SEO), social media posts, newsletters, and word of mouth. Your outbound leads, on the other hand, are usually acquired through paid efforts like ads and cold outreach.

What Is a Sales Funnel?

"Lead" is the term used for a person entering your sales funnel. The typical funnel has between four and six stages. Your sales funnel will be designed to turn your prospects into not only paying customers, but fans.

AWARENESS

Your prospects will enter the awareness phase the moment they first hear about you and your brand. Whether potential customers find you through an ad, a referral, or a social media post, what's important is that they get a clear vision of what you offer and how they can work with you. The goal is to lead them to the next phase, *Interest.* One way to do this is to offer freebies—have prospects follow you on social media or sign up for your newsletter so they can continue to learn about you. Once they do, you can prompt them to sign up for a discovery call, which will be the point at which they shift from being a prospect to a lead.

INTEREST

In the *Interest* phase, they start looking into your competitors and comparing services, prices, and so on. This is where you come in—it's your job to really establish yourself as the expert in your field and get them hooked on your products or services. Really leaning into your Unique Selling Proposition and making sure it's at the forefront of how you position yourself is key.

This is *not* when you want to use a hard sell approach. Try to be as helpful as possible. Remember that providing a great customer experience makes a huge difference in how you'll compare to your competitors and sets a precedent for what it's like to work with you going forward. The trick here is to give them some incentive to enter the *Decision* phase ASAP. This is when you offer them a sales proposition that is exclusive or limited in scope, such as a "limited time only" offer.

DECISION

It's time to make a *Decision*. This is the last phase before money is exchanged; therefore, follow-ups are exceptionally important. If your leads attended a webinar you hosted, try to schedule a fifteen-minute call with them; if you have a promo code to offer, send out an email to remind them. This is also a great time to provide case studies and testimonials.

ACTION

And now, it's time for *Action*. At this point, your leads have decided to pay you. Take a minute to ask yourself, *can I also use this opportunity to*

upsell? Absolutely. Once you've locked in your customer, try to promote an additional service for a reduced rate, or another exclusive or limited time offer.

And congratulations! You have made a sale (or two).

FANS

There is one last step that's often neglected: turning buyers into real *Fans*. These are the people who tell their friends about you—they are your VIPs, your ambassadors. Having your customers feel appreciated builds loyalty, and loyalty grows businesses.

Converting from customer to fan can start with a simple thank-you email that offers an incentive to purchase again and refer a friend. Alternatively, once they have become a customer, ask for feedback. Create a survey or schedule a fifteen-minute call—people often appreciate being heard and value the time you take to hear them out.

How to Create Your Sales Strategy

Having a solid pitch and sales funnel son los primeros pasos, but knowing how to most effectively reach your target audience is what will convert your leads. You of course want to place your pitch in ways that best reach your target audience, and a good way to do that is to develop your buyer persona.

Develop Your Buyer Persona

A buyer persona is a representation of your ideal customer based on your market research. Personas are different from the target audience that you defined in the beginning of your process; they are customer profiles based on your current and potential customers. Some things to consider when building your personas: demographics like location, age, and income, as well as what goals they have, the challenges they face, and their preferred method of communication.

A true understanding of your customers' needs will help you develop more personal messaging that connects in a more direct way than your competitors' messaging. Everyone likes to feel that the services or products they are buying are made with their needs in mind; as a brand builder, that should be your goal.

Once you have your buyer persona written out, you can integrate their pain points into your sales strategy. Try to map your customer's journey. This way, you ensure that you are catering to them at every stage of their decision-making process.

Mapping Your Customer's Journey

Understanding every step of your customer's journey through the sales funnel is essential for effective marketing, especially while you are initially building up your customer base!

The first step to understanding your customer's journey is to map it out—yes, literally draw a map of your sales funnel with the different ways your customers move through it. Fill in the chart on the next page to start you off:

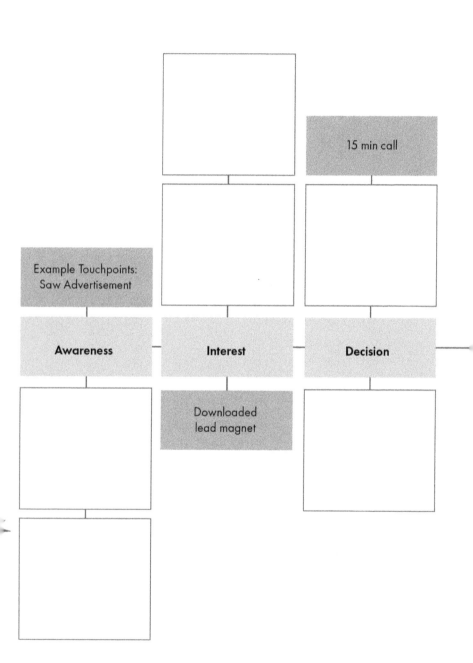

		15 min call
Example Touchpoints: Saw Advertisement		
Awareness	**Interest**	**Decision**
	Downloaded lead magnet	

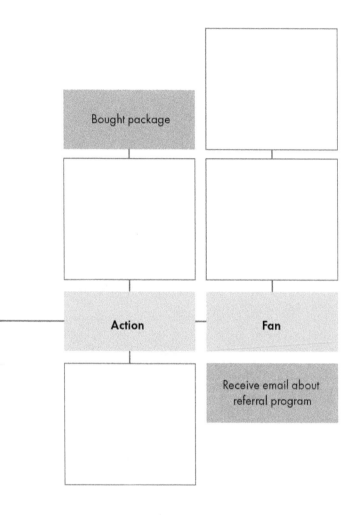

Bought package

Action

Fan

Receive email about
referral program

This process allows you to ask yourself questions that can accelerate your conversion process and improve your rate of lead conversion. Here are some sample questions:

- Does the customer get enough information at each point of contact with your business?

  - Is it easy for customers to find clear information on pricing, or do they have to jump through too many hoops to locate it?

- Is the information you provide relevant to where they are in the funnel?

  - Are you discovering more about customers as they move further along in the funnel? Can you tailor the information you provide them so that it is more personalized?

- Are they waiting more than twenty-four hours to hear back when they make an inquiry? Rapid response times play a huge role in converting leads to sales.

- Are you following up when you notice inactivity from a lead or an existing customer? Haven't heard from them in a while? You should be following up with every lead and existing customer.

What is important to track here are your interactions with potential customers and how they react to them. In most situations, your leads at the top of your funnel will need a little bit more atención (early on, in the Awareness and Interest phases). To increase retention, be sure to stay in regular contact with your customers on their journey.

Por ejemplo, in the case of the tech startup mentioned in Chapter Five, employees noticed how guests who attended one-on-one demos shifted from the Interest phase to the Decision phase more often and more rapidly following a personalized phone call than after an email with a promo code. To test our conversion strategies, we made it a goal to connect with every visitor for a fifteen-minute phone conversation.

Providing clients with a one-on-one feedback session not only gave the startup valuable information about what to improve, it also laid the groundwork for customer retention. More than 50 percent of customers who did one-on-one feedback sessions became returning customers.

This is a good example of how you can get potential customers to stay on track at points where they might otherwise fall out of the funnel. In most cases, you can add different kinds of touchpoints such as automated emails along with other engagement opportunities like webinars and calls to action (reminders to book a call or refer a friend).

It All Starts with Lead Generation

Lead generation is the process of collecting new prospects. Usually a diverse set of marketing tactics is useful in generating leads—you can reach out via email, social media, blog posts, or ads—but lead magnets allow you to capture their information.

Lead magnets are pieces of content you give away for free in exchange for a lead's contact information. Some examples of lead magnets include quizzes, toolkits, checklists, PDF downloads, free trials, discount codes, or even a place on a waitlist for a free consultation. Think of your unique buyer persona. What would interest them? What can you provide that will solve their problems?

Once you have created your lead magnets, create a landing page where your customers can easily find them—a static web page that provides the following:

- Clear details on what you are offering
- The *value* of what they are buying
- A testimonial or two so they can see what investing in this product or service does for you
- How *your* brand is making this a different and desirable experience for them (your Unique Selling Proposition!)
- A specific call to action (e.g., a download or subscription offer)

An example of offering a lead magnet is placing an ad online for a free toolkit download. Once someone clicks on the ad, they are redirected to a landing page that clearly states all of the elements mentioned above.

While you can acquire leads through organic marketing and community building, which we'll cover in the next chapter, the right copy, graphics, audience, and strategy can get the proper leads into your marketing funnel and turn them into paying customers.

Para Más Inspiración: Unos Consejos
Your Mini-Guide to Running Ads

Reyna Marrufo is an LA-based business and marketing coach who specializes in managing Facebook and Instagram ads. She's helped a diverse group of entrepreneurs and now manages over $60,000 a month in paid ads for her clients. Here is a quick guide on how to start running ads that convert!

Before You Run Ads

✧ **Establish a solid social media presence.** Reyna recommends building an engaged social media community and a developed brand. You do not need to have thousands of followers, but make sure you have at least a few quality photos and some content designed to appeal to your target audience. This helps establish credibility.

✧ **Have an idea of what your marketing budget is going to be.** If you decide to hire a Facebook ad manager, you will of course need to pay their service fee in addition to ad costs. The more you invest in advertising, the more campaigns you can test and the more people you can reach.

✧ **Set up your systems to nurture your leads.** Ads are very powerful, and when they are strategically created, they bring leads. It's important to know where you're going to send your initial leads in your marketing funnel after they come in; you don't want them to get left behind. I suggest having a product ready to send or an email campaign in place to help move your leads along.

What Makes a Good Ad?

✧ **A captivating visual and headline:** If you're including a photo, it must be of good quality. To get more engagement on social media ads, consider a video. These stop people from scrolling and prompt interaction.

✧ **Copy that strikes a unique note:** Paid ad copy is different from landing page, website, or social media copy. It's effective to be conversational and use emojis to add some of your personality. The important part is that you address what your audience is struggling with and how your business is the solution.

✧ **Create a sense of urgency:** Setting up a limited-time-only coupon code or exclusive offer motivates leads to take action and not leave it for later.

✧ **Good things take time:** It can take one to two months to finalize an ad based on what's working and what's not. An experienced ad manager will know how to evaluate this and how to try out different image and copy options.

How to Track Your Ads

One of the most important metrics is the Click Through Rate, which shows whether people are engaging with the ad and clicking on the call to action; make sure it is at or above 1 percent. You will also want to track the Cost Per Result, which will vary for each industry and type of business. The goal is to keep the Cost Per Result low and make sure you are profitable.

Mistakes to Avoid

- ✧ **Boosting Posts vs. Creating Ads:** The most common mistake is "boosting" posts instead of creating ads within Facebook Business Manager. These two strategies are quite different, but most importantly, launching an ad within Facebook Business Manager gives you a lot more control than boosting a post.

- ✧ **Not Targeting Your Audience:** Even if you have a great ad, if it is not seen by the right people, it will not convert. You must target the correct audience so that your business will reach people who are willing to invest in it.

- ✧ **Not Spending Enough on Ads:** Usually, people want to use ads to make sales, but asking people to buy your product may turn out to be more expensive than simply promoting your website and garnering views. This is very much the case if your product is expensive.

- ✧ **Changing the Ads Too Soon:** It will take some time to test out what ad copy and visuals work best, so please be patient! It's all about trying out your best ideas, tracking results, and fine-tuning your approach. Also, it is important to not make any changes to your ads for at least a week. Give enough time for the campaign to be noticed and for sufficient data to accumulate so you can see what works.

Make the Most of Your Strategy

Having an efficient sales strategy isn't always just about making the sale. In fact, most of your time will actually be spent getting people into the first few stages of your funnel as well as checking in with the people at the end of your funnel. Retention is just as important as acquisition. In order to take advantage of all leads that come your way, make sure that you are doing the following:

Track and Engage Lost Leads

Even if you get some people telling you "no" (which you will—and that's okay), there is a lot of value in knowing why prospects are not interested. Is it not the right time? Is there something you're not offering? You'll want to keep their information on hand in case you can catch them down the line. Ask them if you can subscribe them to your newsletter so they can stay in the loop about what you offer!

Always Follow Up on Warm Leads

Warm leads are the people who are in the pre-decision phases of your marketing funnel. If you do not have a couple of follow-ups in your pipeline, you may be leaving money on the table. Especially after prospects watch a demo or have been sent a proposal, they may have questions. If these questions are not answered in a timely manner, it may be a deal-breaker. If you are working with representatives of larger clients who must run their decision by their bosses, you'll want to track who needs to be followed up with and when, especially if it's outside your normal follow-up cycle.

Evaluate How Successfully You're Converting

Track how many times you contact your leads before they make a purchase. If you find yourself going back and forth with your leads more than is really necessary, it might be because they are not getting enough information in the early stages of your funnel. To deliver the right facts to them faster, think about what information you can provide by sharing your mission through storytelling strategies, providing case studies, and finding ways to create urgency in the demand for your products or services.

Make Feedback a Part of Your Strategy

Do not be discouraged by bad feedback! Instead, use it to improve your acquisition and retention. If you can get an honest answer as to why your service or product was not a good fit (whether it's the price, user experience issues, or other concerns), then you can get a better sense of how to cater to either a new section of your audience or existing customers. The needs of your audience can change as the world changes, and being in tune with their feedback can help you keep up with what they need!

Check In with Existing Customers

Be sure to add regular quarterly check-ins to your strategy to help with customer retention. For any business, the goal is to develop a loyal following. The truth is, if your customers don't hear from you after their first purchase, then even if they had a great buying experience, they may not feel as inclined to reengage with your business. Not checking in with clients can cause them to drop off completely and/or may make it harder to sell to them in the future. Remember that they have the power to refer people from their networks as well! A little check-in to remind them about an upcoming sale or opportunity may prompt them to make another purchase and/or get some new people into your funnel.

Key Takeaways from Lección 7

* Familiarize yourself with the different phases of your sales funnel.

* Create lead magnets to generate new leads through ads and your other communication pillars.

* Develop at least one buyer persona to help you tailor your offerings to your clientele.

* Map your customers' journey to see where you can communicate with them more efficiently for your sales goals along the way.

* Put focus on acquiring new customers, but don't forget about retaining the old ones. Make their feedback part of your strategy.

* If you run ads, make sure you are targeting the correct audience, budget sufficient funds to give them a chance to work, and be patient with the process of testing them! Track your Click Through Rates for a week, then see what is pulling for you as well as what might not be working.

¡Manos a La Obra!

Creating Buyer Personas

Knowing your buyer personas will not only improve your sales strategy, it will also prepare you to build your community and plan relevant content. Doing your homework on customer profiles will help you create better ways to attract and engage your audience.

Remember that depending on your business, it is possible that you will have multiple buyer personas. You can even include examples of leads who might *not* be a fit. There is no ideal number of buyer personas to create, but if you cater to people in different industries or age groups, you'll want to include one persona for each of those different segments. That way you can look at each persona and integrate them into the development of your product and/or service, sales pitches, and other elements of your marketing.

For now, let's start with two personas. Fill in the boxes below and refer to these if you get stuck in later phases of your launch!

Persona 1 Demographics (Age, Location, Income, Job Title)	Persona 2 Demographics (Age, Location, Income, Job Title)

Goals + Challenges	Goals + Challenges
_____	_____
_____	_____
_____	_____

Favorite Brands/Accounts They Follow	Favorite Brands/Accounts They Follow
_____	_____
_____	_____
_____	_____

What platforms we reach them on? (Social media, email list, webinars, etc.)	What platforms we reach them on? (Social media, email list, webinars, etc.)
_____	_____
_____	_____
_____	_____

"Hablando
se entiende
la gente."

Lección 8

Sigue Creciendo

It is great to have a good product, it's great to sell incredible services, it's great to have a solid brand identity to reflect all of this, and it's great to have a strong sales strategy. What's even better? Having a loyal following—a comunidad to buy from you and support you in other ways, including referring people to you.

In this chapter, we're going to cover how to grow and nurture your community through organic marketing—content, social media engagement, newsletters, and other ways to engage your following. You will use everything you have built so far to find ways to stand out in the digital space and grow your brand.

Growing Your Comunidad

Having a sense of community means that you have built trust between your brand and consumers. Developing that trust will not only give you the ability to reach a larger audience but also help you identify who your VIPs are—some people call them brand ambassadors. They are the ones who will advocate for your brand down the line, and that kind of word of mouth is incredibly powerful.

Thankfully, there are plenty of ways to reach new people in our virtual world, including social media, email, and virtual and in-person events.

We can engage these new contacts using strategies like membership communities and referral programs. While knowing how to use each of these methods of communication is important in terms of knowing what will resonate with your audience, don't forget to observe how your community is engaging with you.

Using Social Media Platforms

Facebook, Instagram, Twitter, TikTok, YouTube, LinkedIn, Clubhouse...is it realistic to think we can keep up with all of these channels *plus* market via email *and* actually run a business?

It is difficult, but not impossible; so therefore, I'm going to tell you to meet your followers and potential consumers where they are. If you know you're mainly going to sell to baby boomers, maybe don't rush over to TikTok; but if you know you want to get on the Gen Z train, start practicing those dance moves.

Social media is great for boosting brand awareness and connecting to your followers in a way that makes them want to continue engaging with you. Though most people won't make purchases directly from social media platforms, following you will keep you at the top of their mind when they are looking for something like what you're offering.

Jefa in Training

Para Más Inspiración: Un Ejemplo

Marivette Navarrete's Five Tips to Growing and Engaging Your Social Media Following

One example of a powerhouse Latina who grew her media brand on social media to over 50,000 followers in just over three years is Marivette Navarrete, founder and CEO of *The Mujerista*. *The Mujerista* has grown to be a recognized community, as well as a platform where Latinas tell their authentic stories and foster connections between one another. The way she consistently puts out engaging content for her comunidad while staying true to her brand is inspiring—this should be the goal for every budding brand's marketing strategy.

Stay True to Your Mission

Become consciously aware of the purpose and values underlying your mission and create quality content that aligns with them. In my case, *The Mujerista* is dedicated to creating an empowering space for Latinas to cultivate new connections and share their stories while proudly showcasing our communities and culture. With this in mind, we create and share content or resources that fit these goals. For example, we share stories and events that highlight Latinas who are making a difference, strengthen our community's sense of positive identity and relationship ties, or provide a connection to our beautiful cultures. Some things we wouldn't share: content that makes fun of our community in an offensive manner or that involves trivial celebrity gossip.

As you are building and creating for your brand, continue to ask yourself why what you're sharing with your community is important for them to see. That way, you'll never go off track. If the content pertains to your mission, then you're set. If not, then it most likely will not interest your audience as they originally engaged with your brand because of the mission you set out to achieve. It's easy to feel that you need to participate and share in the latest trends on social media to gain more followers, but if it's way off base from your goals, then you'll end up alienating or losing the followers who already engage with you.

Create Quality Content

It's not about how often you post or being on top of the latest social media trends. Trendy posts will only give you momentary momentum. It's about creating content that will outlast the trends and speak to your audience, even months after it was posted. Your followers will differentiate you from the rest and treat you as a trusted go-to source. Quality gives your content timelessness. When something is timeless, it rings as true today as it did twenty years ago, and as it will twenty years from now.

Create a Genuine Connection with Your Followers

In this age of social media, people want to feel a connection with brands. *The Mujerista* welcomes people to our community by creating content that is purpose-driven and aligns with their values, allowing them to identify with both the network and others in the community. We utilize our platform to share social causes we believe in and content that speaks to Latinx identities by publishing compelling stories that inspire and bring awareness to the community. By sharing comical memes or cultural posts, we relate to some of our community's shared experiences through different mediums. We make sure that we support our community of Latinas by spotlighting or featuring them in our content, highlighting our strength, beauty, and perseverance.

Again, the kind of content that works best to attract new people to our community is that which stays true to our mission. Our audience engages with us to learn, feel represented, take pride in their cultural

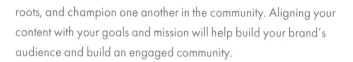

roots, and champion one another in the community. Aligning your content with your goals and mission will help build your brand's audience and build an engaged community.

Invite Your Audience into Your Brand's Journey

Before launching *The Mujerista*, I shared the process of building out the brand with our growing community. They got to watch as I chose logos, font styles, and color palettes, and as I worked on the website and its content. This created excitement around the brand and a deeper connection with *The Mujerista* for our followers. As your brand grows, keep bringing your audience along for the ride. Share posts where you are doing things like dropping off customer packages at the post office, engaging in the process of creating a new product, or hosting an event. Be raw and honest; share the good and the bad, the highs and the lows. This empowers your audience to feel what you feel, root for you, and identify with those moments in their own lives.

Be Supportive of Others in Your Community or Industry

The Mujerista stands behind the idea of comunidad over competition. Use your platform to highlight others in your space who are creating something amazing—give them a voice and share their work.

Creating Content

Regardless of what goes on with social media algorithms, the content we post is not only for follower growth but also for retention. In order to help narrow down what to post, it is helpful to think about setting up different pillars of content (also known as content buckets). Based on these, you will come up with ideas on what to post, making the process intentional and strategic. The platform on which you choose to post will depend on the audience you want to see it and the format in which you want them to see it.

For most of you, the following general content bucket definitions may work:

▶ **Promotion**: Be mindful of using your social media for strictly promotion; you will want to make promo posts no more than 20 percent of your weekly posts.

▶ **Expertise**: These posts show you know what you're doing; provide tips, testimonials, and how-tos.

▶ **Lifestyle**: People want to see that you are human, and they want to be able to relate to you in some way.

▶ **Thought-Leadership**: Make posts in which you share resources, give recaps of events you've hosted, and recount lessons you've learned. For example, If I am a coach who hosts a weekly accountability group, and once a week I like to promote one of my services, I could talk about this group in a few different ways:

- Write an article for LinkedIn on why accountability groups are important

- Create a short video (to post on Instagram Reels or TikTok) on the five benefits of joining an accountability group

- Highlight case studies of clients who have been able to level up their businesses because of weekly accountability groups on Instagram or on my blog

- Feature testimonials in an appealing post on social media

Jefa in Training

You will want to take an idea and stretch it out in various ways to create content that people will see, understand, and want more of after following you! Aside from posting on social media, you will also want to start considering setting up an email marketing plan.

Email Marketing Is Not Dead

According to a 2021 study by Constant Contact,[1] 60 percent of consumers say they've made a purchase as a result of a marketing email they received, compared to the 12.5 percent of consumers who have considered using the "buy" button on social media.

You can get to people faster through email; you avoid having to deal with social media algorithms, and you can still get them when they are on the go, as mobile devices account for 60 percent of emails opened in 2021. There have also been several brands that started off solely as newsletters and have built full-fledged media brands from that starting point.

Para Más Inspiración: Unos Consejos
Three Things to Know About Starting a Newsletter with Lila Miller

Bonita Semana is a weekly newsletter in Spanish as well as an online platform and community created by and for career- and wellness-focused Latinx. It was created by Lila Miller, a Mexican-born, Brooklyn-based designer, illustrator, and editor who wanted to feel closer to her Latinx heritage after moving from Monterrey to New York City. Her dream was to have a huge online community, but as a team of one, a newsletter was a good first step. Founded in 2017, the newsletter now

---

1   blogs.constantcontact.com/email-marketing-statistics

has over 20,000 subscribers and Bonita Semana has over 30,000 followers on Instagram. She plans to start hosting events and providing even more content for its audience.

Write about Something You Like and Be Vulnerable

People react best to words that come from a place of honesty and vulnerability. Our readers seem to connect deeply with what we have to say because it turns out we're all just trying to figure things out. We only share things that we really like, projects that excite us, and interesting articles that make us think. No filters please!

Make Your Newsletter Easily Shareable

Referrals have been great for us—if people like what you do, they share it with their friends, and that's the best kind of promotion anyone could aspire to have. We also use social media to indirectly promote the newsletter with inspirational quotes, illustrations, and screenshots of what we have in store.

Keep It Simple and Consistent

When it comes to design, a simple one goes a long way, and consistency truly is key!

Marketing through email not only helps to both grow brand awareness and drive sales with your subscribers, it also gives you a unique opportunity to evoke those key community-building feelings we talked about earlier: the experience of being heard, appreciated, and special. Offer them exclusive opportunities like promo codes, a first look at new products, and early access to events. You can also create special content like worksheets or podcast episodes—things that are low-cost for you but high-value to them.

Create Community via Social Media and Email

Many content creators, whether they are musicians, writers, service-based entrepreneurs, or even content workers at tech and media startups, have found the value in launching membership subscription communities in order to boost their brand's engagement—and yes, many even count on it as another revenue stream. Especially during COVID-19, when so many have shifted from hosting in-person events and sought more ways to captivate and interact with their following, having an online space to connect off of social media and create more of an exclusive and intimate experience with perks for your community is a win-win for everyone!

Launching a Membership Community

If this is something you think you would want to explore, here are some things to think about first:

1: WHO IS YOUR TARGET AUDIENCE?

We've already gone over the importance of this question, but it is entirely relevant and important to community-building, especially if you're hoping to launch an entire platform dedicated to more hands-on work to engage with your members. How will they respond to a membership setting? Will they be interested in connecting in this way?

2: WHAT VALUE WILL YOU BE PROVIDING TO YOUR COMMUNITY?

With the launch of so many virtual memberships, Slack networks, and so on, it's important to know what you will be providing for your community besides a virtual space to meet like-minded individuals. Some things to consider are hosting virtual events, regular hours when you're available for complimentary one-on-one appointments, providing exclusive content, access to courses, and partnerships with other like-minded brands for discounts and free products. Consistently offering value is what will get your members to see your community as a valued resource and keep them coming back.

3: WHAT PLATFORM WILL YOU USE?

Depending on how you answered questions 1 and 2, there are a few different routes you can go here. The simplest strategy, which I think is necessary regardless of whether you intend to have an additional platform, is a combination of developing engaging content and putting it out through social media and email newsletters. However, if your goal is to get off of social media and away from the everyday emails your public may be getting, you can look into additional platforms that are designed to build online communities, like Facebook Groups, Slack, Mighty Networks, Discord, OwnTrail, and Circle.io. If you are more creative and frequently create content like music, videos, or articles, then perhaps Patreon, a hybrid membership community and crowdfunding platform, could be a good option for you. There are pros and cons to each platform, so check each one out and do some research not only on what would be easiest for your community, but on what features you will need to best engage with them as well.

4: HOW WILL YOU GET YOUR FIRST GROUP OF MEMBERS?

Do you already have a newsletter or a social media following? If not, the first step would be to tap into some other networks to find your ideal members and invite them to become part of your beta test group. If you are launching a paid platform, you can offer a free trial for a certain amount of time or a reduced-price founding membership that can include additional perks and privileges down the line.

5: HOW WILL YOU KEEP THEM ENGAGED ONCE THEY HAVE JOINED?

For those of you who already have a following, the previous questions may have been easy for you. Here is where you will have to do more work, especially if you're going into this as a solopreneur! It is essential that someone (whether it is you or another person) covers community management tasks for your new network, including:

▶ Making sure each new member is welcomed and answering their questions

▶ Encouraging members to connect with each other and facilitating conversations

▶ Implementing programming on behalf of your brand (i.e., providing value to members)

Find Ways to Engage

Through all the social media platforms, email, and other technology we rely on to collect data on customer engagement, it's easy to forget the most important fact we can use to connect with our community: *We are all human.* When we think about it that way, it seems obvious that we need to take into consideration how our supporters are feeling. When they feel they are much more than just a number on your Instagram follower count or your newsletter subscriber list, that's what will keep them coming back to you.

Here are three things to think about as you build your community strategy:

▶ **Make Them Feel Heard**: Especially when you are first starting out, ask your supporters for feedback on whatever it is you're doing. It's part of the process, and it will help you improve your offerings in the long run. After all, if you are growing a community, who better to listen to than your community!

▶ **Make Them Feel Appreciated**: Send out regular updates on where you are in your journey. People like hearing about progress, especially if they are giving you money. Create a rewards program for them to save money, get a free product or service, post shout-outs on social media—let them know you are grateful for their support!

▶ **Make Them Feel Special**: Physical rewards are great, but sometimes people just like having a sense of being valued by someone they are supporting. Try giving them responsibility—like inviting them to be a guest on your podcast, featuring their reviews on social media, or encouraging them to meet with you to give you their feedback.

All of this will help you get them to become actively engaged with you, maintain that connection, and foster brand devotion. Remember: 1,000 actively engaged community members is far better than 10,000 who never show up.

Key Takeaways from Lección 8

* Remember that we are all human, and when building your community strategy, keep these feelings in mind as you reach out to your supporters: Heard, Appreciated, Supported.

* Meet your followers and potential consumers on social media platforms where they are.

* Producing social media content that works for your brand is about creating content that speaks to your audience, even months after posting. Go beyond the trends; your followers will see how you are different from the rest and learn to trust you as a go-to source. Quality gives your content timelessness.

* For newsletters: People react best to words that come from a place of honesty and vulnerability. Write about something you like, and your content will attract new people; a simple design goes a long way and consistency is truly key.

¡Manos a La Obra!

Create Your Content Planner

Now that you've learned what kind of content to focus on and what channels you may want to use to start, let's get them down on paper and make a schedule. Content planning can be time-consuming, so having a schedule can be really helpful—especially if and when you start outsourcing design and copywriting.

Here's a chart to get you started, but you can always create this same form in an Excel spreadsheet as an example or in an online content planner of your choosing.

> "Spontaneity is beautiful, but planning is genius. In a social media world filled with clutter and beautiful images, it takes taking a step back to figure out your voice and your audience to bring to life a social media plan that is successful. Be true to your voice, be fun, and always focus on the problem you're trying to solve. People don't want to be sold a product, they want to walk with you in that product discovery journey."
>
> —Marlene Ramirez, Senior Manager for Brand Partnerships at PLANOLY

Date	Type of Post + Platform	Image	Copy + Hashtags	Notes
4/1/22	Response to article LinkedIn	N/A	*Link to Article* I feel that this is... #business #womeninbiz	Tag author of original article
4/2/22	Video/Reel Instagram	Five different books that inspired my journey	Each one of these has left a mark on me and has inspired me to... #booksofig #writersofig	Tag authors
4/3/22	Carousel	Introducing My New Business—Here's what I offer	DM me to learn more!	

"Palo solo no hace monte."

Lección 9

Promoción y Colaboración

In the last chapter, we covered the basics of organic marketing—efforts you can make on your own to start building your comunidad and getting awareness of your new venture out there to the right people. While genuinely connecting with your audience through your own communication channels (i.e., social media and email) is important, it is not the only way to reach and engage them.

In this chapter, our focus is going to be on things you can do to help promote your brand by working with other people while at the same time building some outside credibility for your business and establishing yourself as a leader in your industry. We'll start with the basics of public relations (aka PR): the benefits and some how-tos. Then we'll go into partnerships and how to leverage them in building your brand.

Let's Talk About PR

Public relations, publicity, whatever you want to call it—not only does it get your name out there to new audiences, it also establishes credibility within your industry. I mean, who doesn't want to say they've been featured in *Forbes*, *Entrepreneur*, *The New York Times*, and so on!

So what does it take to get featured in news media and magazines as well as blogs and podcasts? It's a balance between strategy, relationships, and a good story.

The difference between marketing and PR is that you sometimes have to pay for marketing (e.g., ads, influencer marketing, and paid partnerships). PR, however, is built largely on relationships you cultivate with writers, editors, podcasters, and producers, as well as social media accounts that feature stories about your industry. If you are just starting to get out there and build those relationships, it's also about having a good pitch.

~~~~~~

Para Más Inspiración: Unos Consejos

Four Ways to Attract Press from Danielle Alvarez

Danielle Alvarez, publicist for many beauty and fashion brands and founder of The Bonita Project, says that when pitching, it's important to know how to best position yourself.

Before You Pitch

✧ Pay attention to how you are pitching yourself. What are you bringing to the table that no one else can? What kind of credibility do you have that makes you stand out?

✧ Do your research on who you are pitching to make sure your story is a good fit. Does your brand's image fit in with who they have featured in the past?

PR Is Changing—To Keep Up, Be Authentic

Now that we live in such a social-media-driven world, traditional PR almost takes a back seat. If you have to pick between investing in PR or investing in social media, invest in your social media first because your online presence matters in PR.

Your follower count does not matter as much as attracting an engaged community by being authentic. People are paying more attention to where they are spending their dollars, and they want to see brands that show they are authentic and inclusive. If you represent that on social media, you'll have a better chance at landing a feature.

Think Outside the Box

Gone are the days of just pitching for an article in a magazine or blog— PR has evolved to include not only working closely with influencers to spread the word about your brand and products but collaborating with bigger social media accounts. An example of a current collab would be doing an Instagram Live with an influencer. Sometimes you'll get more traction by doing this than from having been featured in an article because of the direct engagement you can have with people watching.

Make It Easy

When you are writing your pitch, you can always include a press release, but it's important to personalize your email as much as possible. A good subject line is an absolute must. Pro tip: Include a bulleted list of the topics you can cover during an interview or featured article. Most of these editors get hundreds of emails each day, so it is your job to make it easy for them to be intrigued by what they are reading.

While you can hire a publicist who has years of experience with pitching and relationships, that will require a budget that some of you may not have right away. If you cannot afford one, that doesn't mean that PR is off the table. But while it won't be costly in dollars, it can take up a lot of your time.

6 Steps Para Obtener Publicidad

Based on my own experience pitching as well as the insight of a couple of writers in the industry (thank you, Vivian Nunez and Marilyn La Jeunesse), here are five steps along with best practices to start getting publicity for your business:

Step 1: Do Your Research

Just as you did your market research, you'll also want to research the outlets and the writers to whom you plan to pitch. Do not pitch a story about politics to someone who writes about beauty—the email will just get skipped over. Know what their niche is, and research how they want to be contacted. Do not contact people via direct messages on their social media profiles unless they say otherwise.

Step 2: Personalize Your Pitch

Do not copy and paste your pitches—writers will know when you've sent about a hundred other writers the same thing (especially if you forget to personalize your email and leave the wrong name in the greeting). It is easier for writers to latch on to your idea if you tie it to what you already know about them.

Step 3: Before You Send, Be Conscious of Timing

Try not to send anything during off-hours or holidays, and be sensitive to current events. If there's a national tragedy happening, it's best to hold off on unrelated pitches that are not time-sensitive and can wait at least forty-eight hours.

Jefa in Training

Step 4: When Pitching via Email, Get to the Point Sooner Rather Than Later

▶ Use direct and to-the-point subject lines like: "New: [Product] [Brand]" or "Exclusive Opportunity: [Person]"

▶ Write the reason for your pitch in the first few lines: Why should they cover this? How is this pitch unique? Is this an exclusive?

▶ In your email to a writer you're pitching, make your ask very clear: How they could include your brand in a listicle, a review, or an interview? However, don't assume that they can do a long-form piece, as that's not always the case.

Step 5: Press Releases Are Sent Upon Request

Most writers will only ask for a press release if they need it. Do not send it with your immediate outreach email as an attachment because your email will have a greater chance of ending up in someone's spam folder.

Here are some press release basics:

▶ Your title should be short and sweet, but captivating to the reader.

▶ The first paragraph should include all basic information—the who, what, where, when, and why.

▶ The second paragraph should go further into the "how."

▶ You should also include a quote from the founder or whoever the release is talking about.

▶ In the closing paragraph, tie it together with any other important relevant information (what is coming next and where they can learn more).

▶ At the end of your press release, be sure to let them know who they can contact for more information or to set up a feature.

Step 6: Be Aware of Follow-Ups

Some writers appreciate follow-ups if they are not excessive. If something is time-sensitive for you, that does not mean it's time-sensitive for them. And if you have not heard back after a second or third follow-up, a fourth one is not going to help.

~~~~~~

Para Más Inspiración: Un Ejemplo

Within just a year of launching her business, Bonita Fierce Candles, Melissa Gallardo went on to be featured in major outlets like *Cosmopolitan*, Univision, BeLatina, Luz Collective, and *The Mujerista*. Melissa says that her sales nearly doubled within the first month after each of her features—a huge win for her new small business!

Here's one tip she shares when it comes to PR for small businesses:

> It's so hard to gain exposure when you don't have an established social media following—but what will help you is to join like-minded communities where you can network with people who will help support you!

Actively post about your business because you never know who is paying attention. The writer of the *Cosmo* article heard about Bonita Fierce Candles through a friend of Melissa's from college. Do not underestimate the power of word of mouth!

Here is the formula and an example pitch we used to successfully land placements for *ABC News*, *Good Housekeeping*, and more!

Subject Line: Straight to the point—say who you are and what you want

First Paragraph: Quien eres y why they should keep reading (que te distingue?)

Second Paragraph: Details of the request

Third Paragraph: Where they can find more info and how to contact you

Example:

Subject: Latin-Inspired Bonita Fierce Candles Feature Request for Hispanic Heritage Month

Hi [Name Of Person],

I'm Melissa! The founder of Bonita Fierce Candles, a Latina-owned small business that celebrates heritage and home through eco-conscious candles. With Hispanic Heritage Month approaching, I'm celebrating by putting a spotlight on my signature line of candles, which includes scents like "Abuela's Bakery" and "Cafecito Con Leche." I'm reaching out to you today to see if you are working on any features of Latinx-owned businesses that Bonita Fierce could be a part of.

We've previously been featured in *Cosmopolitan*, *The Mujerista*, The Luz Collective, and BeLatina News and we'd love it if we could be featured in [insert outlet name here] this fall!

You can find out more about the different candles and our sustainability efforts here [insert link].

Hope to hear from you and collaborate soon! Happy to send any other information you need!

Best Regards,
Melissa Gallardo

3 Ways to Spice Up Your PR Strategy

As Danielle mentioned earlier, being creative with your PR strategy could be what gets you attention. Starting to develop those relationships now with people who cover stories in your industry is a good start, but there are other ways that you can actually pitch yourself to initiate some buzz.

Write Guest Posts!

If you have a knack for writing and you're having trouble getting a writer to cover your story for a specific outlet, see if they accept guest posts. You could switch up the angle of what you were hoping to pitch and make it a first-person narrative. For example: If you are launching an artist management company, instead of publishing a press release about who you are, what you do, and who you work with, you could publish a piece on what artist management means in the current state of the industry.

Do a Social Media Takeover!

Ask a brand's social media account manager if your brand can take over their social media account for a set amount of time. You could offer valuable content to their audience based on your expertise during that time through a live Q and A session, a "day in the life," or a whole Instagram TV episode if you prefer.

Collaborate!

Do an interview with someone on social media, or explore other ways to create a brand partnership.

Partnerships

PR does tend to convert more in comparison to ads because it's organic, but another tactic to add to your promotional strategy is collaboration with like-minded brands. A strategic partnership is when two or more brands collaborate to create a campaign to increase awareness and acquisition—ideally, a win-win para todos. Cultivating partnerships is another authentic way to boost awareness of your brand, as well as establish and scale long-term relationships with other brands in your industry.

Who to Work With?

Partner with brands who cater to the same audience as you—their followers will hopefully become your new followers and vice versa. With a collaborative as opposed to competitive mindset, you will be able to reach more people in a new way. Remember that no one is doing exactly what you are doing, exactly the way you are doing it, so you should not worry about someone "stealing" your followers. That's why it is important to engage your audience and be conscious of their needs.

Ways to Colaborar

Depending on the needs, goals, and bandwidth of each party in a collaboration, you can choose to work with another brand in a few different ways. When you first approach a brand with which you want to partner, get an idea of what their goals are and put together a plan specifying the campaign's goals, with deliverables assigned to each partner. That way, you can look back and assess if the partnership was successful and if you want to try something again down the line.

For the following examples, I'll refer to my organization, #WomxnCrush Music.

CREATE CONTENT AND/OR EVENTS TOGETHER

One way to work with another brand is to cocreate content that will live on the newsletter, blog, social media pages, and/or website of one or both brands. This can be an introductory way to test a longer-term partnership to see if there is mutual interest from each other's audience, depending on how the people in their network engage with the content.

For example, #WomxnCrush Music could curate a virtual tour with performances that would live on another brand's YouTube or Twitch channel, with their team producing it. The benefits for the other company would be that #WCM would do the legwork of scouting artists and getting sponsors to pay the artists, as well as the social good aspect of promoting a nonprofit. The benefits for #WCM would be that this other brand's livestream channel would have a much larger reach with many viewers, and that they would absorb the costs of a virtual producer. The livestream recordings could live on this other brand's website,

and artists could share the recordings with their followers afterward, resulting in even more visibility for both #WCM and our hypothetical "Brand Y."

SHARE LEADS

If Brand Y was, let's say, a music technology company interested in a more direct way to pitch the #WCM community after this event, part of the agreement could be that they would have to share the list of emails of everyone who RSVP'd to each livestream show. While the #WCM community would be smaller than Brand Y's preexisting reach, it would get them access to a different audience that could very well benefit from their product.

PROVIDE VALUABLE OFFERS

If Brand Y requested access to all of #WCM's contacts, they could, in return, provide a limited-time free membership or generous discount for the people on the list. Since part of the mission of #WCM is to provide our community with resources, having access to the platform at a discounted rate would greatly benefit the organization.

CROSS-PROMOTION

Alternatively, no offers, or lead lists, or content have to be shared if there isn't the bandwidth to do so. Some of the most successful partnerships #WCM has done have been purely promotional. A partner could sign on to promote a series of events on their social media and in their newsletter, and we in turn could write about them in our blog and highlight them in our newsletter.

BRAND PARTNERSHIPS AND SPONSORSHIPS

Once you have created a community, you'll be able to leverage brand partnerships not only as a way to get better known out there, but also as a way to generate revenue. Brands hoping to target your audience may offer to give you a certain amount of money to create campaigns introducing their products and services to your followers. In the case of sponsorships, they are paying for ad space at your event, on your flyers, on web pages, and so on.

~~~~~~

Para Más Inspiración: Unos Consejos
Three Tips for Creating Successful Brand Partnerships from Ana Flores

Ana Flores, founder of WeAllGrow Latina, has established several impactful partnerships over the last few years that have both helped increase brand awareness of WeAllGrow and truly benefited her community in a major way. WeAllGrow Latina has partnered with companies like Neutrogena, Audible, Dove, and many others!

It All Starts with a Relationship

Not every interaction is about a dollar sign, and while we do need to know our worth and get paid for our work, there is also a lot of value in building long-term relationships. A great example is Neutrogena; before they became WeAllGrow's title sponsor for their annual WeAllGrow Latina summit, we had worked together on various blog and Instagram campaigns. In the beginning, we sometimes even did things for free because we were just starting to build that relationship.

Jefa in Training

The Neutrogena rep and I both continued to nurture the relationship over time until it grew into something bigger.

You Must Have Proof of Concept

It was easier to get them to jump on board for the summit because they had worked with us in the past for years and felt comfortable working with us. Even though the summit was a new idea, they took the risk with us because they knew that their target audience would be reached through this, just like with the other campaigns we had done. Having a big sponsor like Neutrogena also proved to other sponsors that if Neutrogena trusts us with their investment, they could also be successful in a partnership with us—another proof of concept.

If we had gone in without having that prior relationship, that would have been a different story. When you go in to pitch a partner, you have to arm them with as much information and data as you can—strong messaging and information on how your partnership will help them reach their target audience.

Acknowledge the Goals of the Partnership

Sometimes a partnership will be the right fit, and other times you might have to say no. You have to know the goals of each party in the partnership, and to do that you have to ask the right questions. What is your partner's definition of success—is it a specific rate of return on investment? On your end, you have to know what your audience is looking for. Are they searching for educational content? Inspiration? Does that fall in line with what the partner offers? If not—better to pass than to fail to deliver to your community.

Can you name five like-minded brands you would want to collaborate with in the future? Brainstorm what kind of partnership you would want to pitch to them here:

_____

_____

_____

_____

_____

_____

_____

Collaborate Con Tu Comunidad

In the last chapter, we spoke about growing your comunidad—but I am a strong believer in not only growing your comunidad but allowing them to be a part of your growth journey as well! While brand partnerships are a great way to reach new audiences, finding ways to work with the people who are already loyal to you (and those who have the potential to be loyal to you) will help with both acquisition and retention.

A recent success story of a brand that took over the internet by using ambassadors is Cami Tellez's brand, Parade. Parade sent free samples of their underwear to over six thousand women and nonbinary users of

Instagram (ranging from micro-influencers to celebrities to casual users of the platform) in exchange for social media posts.

This product launch campaign was extremely effective, and the brand also set a trend that has continued, with one in eight Parade customers posting pictures in their new underwear without being asked.

As shown by Parade's example, your ambassadors will be the ones who tag you on social media and frequently make purchases from you. There are a couple of ways you can use that to expand your reach—as long as you can provide them incentives to keep their interest.

Developing Your Brand Ambassador Program

Brand ambassador programs have become popular with beauty and fashion brands; a brand will often have their ambassadors apply to be part of their program. The programs generally offer generous discounts on products, access to early releases, invitations to exclusive events, and cross-promotion of content created by the ambassadors to expand their own following as well. Mission-driven brands like Sozy, founded by Lanai Moliterno, empower their brand ambassadors to spread awareness of causes the brand supports—10 percent of Sozy's profits go to support survivors of sexual violence, with an additional 10 percent supporting other charitable and environmental initiatives.

Brand Ambassadors vs. Loyalty Programs

While brand ambassadors are great to help get the word out, you must vet them, and it might take some time to actually find the right people to represent your brand online. Loyalty or referral programs that give a chance for all of your customers to share your offers with their friends are also a great way to give back to the people who love your brand (but may not want to create content for you).

Some ideas for these kinds of programs are:

- For every friend an existing customer refers, they get X dollars and their friend gets 30 percent off.

- Have a reward system with a point scheme: the more they buy, the more points they accumulate—points are redeemable for discounts or free products!

- Start a *Founding VIP Member* program that locks in your current discounted pricing for these customers and the people they refer in the future.

In the same way as with PR and brand partnerships, working with your community can get you leads who will trust you more because someone they personally know told them about you.

Key Takeaways from Lección 9

* PR is a balance between strategy, relationships, and a good story.

* It is important to know how to best position yourself to the person to whom you are pitching. Do your research.

* Cultivating partnerships is another authentic way to boost brand awareness, as well as establish and scale long-term relationships with other brands in your industry.

* Decide on mutual goals in a partnership and create a plan based on the availability and resources of both partners.

* Collaborating with your community through a brand ambassador program or offering them rewards for referrals can be very powerful for your brand!

* Focus on being authentic and spreading your story throughout— that doesn't change, only the angle of how you pitch it does.

¡Manos a La Obra

Who's On Your Outreach List?

To better prepare for launch, in this ejercicio, you will start creating an outreach plan. The timeline to get information to a media outlet will vary depending on factors including whether it's online or print—but generally, a good rule of thumb is to send it at least a month before any kind of launch. In between launches, you can use partnerships to keep the buzz going!

You can make a media spreadsheet that looks like this and use one sheet for outlets, one for podcasts, and one for partnerships—or do it by whatever method works for you!

Outlet/Podcast/ Partnership Name + Contact Name	Email Address	Date Pitched	Notes

"Empoderar a las mujeres significa confiar en ellas."

-Isabel Allende

Lección 10

Ponte Las Pilas

As someone who went from being a solo socialpreneur to leading a team of thirty volunteers within less than a year, I can tell you firsthand that some parts of leadership will come naturally while others will be learned through experience, either through your own or through experiences passed on to you by a mentor. And by "experience," I am also saying that sometimes you will learn by not always getting things right the first time—and that's okay.

In this chapter, we are going to dive into what it takes to home in on your inner jefa by focusing on different ways to lead the one person who is going to be the center of your business—yourself. Once you have learned how to carve out your path, we will get into some basics of thought leadership and how to share what you offer with the world.

Let's begin with one key question: What is leadership, and how does it affect us if we do not have a team just yet?

Unleashing Your Inner Jefa

Leadership is a process: it is the act of influencing others, yet ultimately, it is an art. There are many aspects to leading well, and a lot of the time, it is subjective; but great leaders do what great art does—they influence

people and help them feel happy, safe, and supported. And that's what you will aim to do as the founder of your business.

You know that quote from *Spiderman* where his uncle says, "With great power comes great responsibility"? He might as well have been talking about starting a business, because not only does being a founder mean that now you have something of your own, it also there is no one else who is responsible for what you're building. That sense of sole responsibility can be intimidating and a little disorienting, especially if you have never experienced it before. But have no fear, jefas—you are almost there.

Como Ser Lider

As a solopreneur, you may be going it alone for the foreseeable future, so it is important that you remember that whenever you are talking to someone, you *are* your brand. Anything that you say or do is going to be associated with it. That is why even when you are first starting out, you must learn how to *earn* the leadership title. You are an entrepreneur and founder by default, but getting people to trust you and to see you as an authority in your industry is another matter—that is something you have to build up as you build your business.

Keep these leadership values in mind on your journey:

STICK TO YOUR "WHY"

It's not always going to be easy to stay motivated. When times get tough and you have to make difficult decisions, remind yourself of why you started this business. Think about the values you set when you were

building your brand and the impact that you wanted to have. Take a look at everything you've built so far, and if things aren't going the way you expected, sit down and answer some of the questions you asked yourself in the beginning—have the answers changed? Evaluate all of the pieces until you can find the best way of bringing your "why" back to the world.

HOLD YOURSELF ACCOUNTABLE

This applies not just to checking things off a to-do list every day, but to holding yourself accountable; this is essential, especially when you make mistakes. Being in a position of leadership doesn't mean you can overlook your own mistakes—it means that you can acknowledge them and take action so that they don't happen again. Even if you don't have a team yet, people are going to look to you for direction, and you have to be fair and hold yourself accountable the same way you'd hold someone else accountable.

LEARN TO FILTER OTHERS' CRITICISM

There are likely going to be times when people do not agree with your decisions on what direction you want to go with your business, how you're promoting your brand on social media, or what font you're using in your branding—and the list goes on. The point is that you are not going to be able to cater to everyone all the time. Starting a business is a vulnerable process; by putting yourself out there, you may also expose yourself to some criticism. Don't let unconstructive criticism weigh you down and waste your time.

BE OPEN TO FEEDBACK

You will start to learn the difference between criticism and constructive criticism—and I want to point out that listening to constructive criticism will actually help you grow. Too many founders make the mistake of thinking they know everything there is to know about their industry and about how to run their business. But once you have been in business for a while, it can be easy to get into a rut with your own way of doing things, and sometimes that has to change.

LET PEOPLE IN

On that note, know when it is time to ask for help. Entrepreneurship is a journey, one that comes with a lot of fulfillment but also a lot of hard work. You do not have to do it alone. There is this misconception that if we seek help, hire coaches, or outsource, we are not strong enough on our own to handle our business—let that go.

In fact, knowing what and how to outsource and delegate is an especially important leadership skill to learn just on its own—and it is the only way to grow. At some point or another, you as the founder are going to have to learn to let go of your biz baby and let someone take over the day-to-day tasks so that you can focus on growth.

Para Más Inspiración: Unos Consejos

Six Tips for Developing the Leadership Mindset from Paulette Pinero

Paulette Pinero is the founder of LEAD Media, a coaching and consulting company that specializes in developing leadership skills in entrepreneurs and managers. As an entrepreneur who coaches other entrepreneurs to be leaders, Paulette says that true authentic leadership comes from the inside out. Along with allowing yourself to be self-aware

Jefa in Training

when it comes to your goals, your purpose, and your mistakes, she also says that it is important for entrepreneurs to have the following mindset and skills to succeed with their launch.

Get Comfortable with Being Uncomfortable

As an entrepreneur, you need to be open to things you haven't done in the past. At work, you focus on your strengths and perhaps put some effort into improving your growth areas, but in business, you learn to do a wide range of things (even if you also hire someone else to do them). Selling, customer service, bookkeeping, going live on social media, networking, talking to prospective clients, documenting your work, emailing, billing—you have to do it all.

One of the things I get the most during coaching sessions is, "I can't sell, I don't have that gene;" my response is, "Then you need to learn." Just like strengthening a muscle, you have to create a plan, start small, and build that skill with time and effort. It's going to be uncomfortable at first, but it gets better if you keep working on it and seek support.

Be Open to Change and Be Ready to Pivot

Remember that fancy business plan you wrote before securing high-ticket clients? Know that your business might look completely different a year from now. Why? Because a good entrepreneur goes where their clients want to go.

When I launched LEAD Media, my plan was to do 70 percent consulting, 25 percent coaching, and 5 percent public speaking. I built a website that spoke to the decision makers at large companies and nonprofits. But I soon realized that mid-level career Latinas who wanted to develop their leadership abilities or launch service-based businesses were the people who wanted to chat with me. That small percentage of a single market segment from my business plan turned out to be

who was engaging most with my content and scheduling clarity and discovery calls with me. I also realized that selling to a company can take weeks, even months, as opposed to selling to individuals, which usually happens in two to three meetings. I had to go back to my business plan, develop strategic priorities, and rebrand my business. Even though I had validated my business idea before launching, the market and other external factors were too unpredictable for me to control every variable, so I changed my priorities, and by doing so, quickly found success

Never Forget That Your Time Is Money

Every minute you spend with a prospect or future client is a piece of your time that you are investing in that relationship, thereby earning your right to stay in the conversation. That also means that you need to learn what their problem is and see if they are the right fit to work with you. You do not have to say yes to every prospect or lead; building a network of similar entrepreneurs will help you refer folks out who are not the right match for you. Have a list of clarity questions on hand, and if you're still unsure after answering them, it's okay to let them go into the "lost" stage of your pipeline.

Get Over Perfectionism

This is the kryptonite of every emprendedora, and the most difficult challenge for most of us. We were raised to work harder, get the best grades, and try to excel at everything we do, but I'm sorry to tell you that perfection is a myth. It took me two and a half years to launch my business because everything had to be perfect—the business plan, the logo, the website—and two things happened: 1) Nothing was ever perfect, because I changed and the market changed, and worst of all, 2) I postponed my dreams for years. Start with what you already have and launch small. Focus on your value proposition and knowing who your customers are. Don't have a website? Start a blog and a social media account. Want a customer relations management system? Consider using Salesforce CRM services for small businesses as you manage your first client experiences. Start with one to two products and services for your key client(s), talk about the value of what you provide, and share how you resolve their problem. When you want to be "perfect," you invest in things you don't need without really knowing what your client wants from you. Also, you don't need a perfect social media feed with all the "perfect" colors and images—just tell your authentic story and show up.

When It Comes to Setting Boundaries...

Whether at home or at your business, let people know what type of relationship you want them to have with you. If you respond to emails at ten o'clock at night when your work or business hours end at four o'clock, why would you be surprised when a client says you are unreachable when you take more than twenty-four hours to respond to their requests? (Hit that "schedule send" button right now!) Whether you manage them or they manage you, let the people you work with know what they can expect from you and by when. When you are managing staff, you should always talk about your schedule, your response time, how and when you make decisions, and when the team or involved individuals will be consulted. As a business owner, you do this with your team, but you also need to check these boxes with your clients. If you are a service-based entrepreneur, a welcome guide or a video outlining expectations for working together is helpful. For product businesses, your website, marketing, and social media all need to let people know what they can expect from the product, the purchase experience, and even the shipping process. Make your boundaries and expectations accessible to everyone, and review them as many times as you need to with others.

Build Your Board of Advisors

The difference between your advisors and a board of directors is that those who occupy those board positions have decision-making power, even if we disagree with them, but your advisors can give you feedback, make connections, and of course, give you advice so you can decide how to move forward. These are the folks who will open doors for you with their connections and will talk about your strengths and achievements when you are not in the room. They are frequently not just advisors, but champions.

Your advisors will be people you meet with about once a quarter to talk about the main pain points on which you need advice. An advisor's purpose for you can be as specific as having an advisor for investing, or marketing, or work-life balance—and it may be important to clarify with each potential advisor what you need from them to see if they can help! Do you want to meet quarterly? Do you hope to do this for six months, one year, or longer? Do you want to spend thirty minutes or an hour each time you confer?

Can you name five people to be on your board of advisors for this next phase of your life and business? Try reaching out to them this week and start building your team!

_____

_____

~~~~~~

Leading yourself is only half the challenge—the other half is proving to the rest of the world that you truly are a jefa in your industry. The next step is to establish yourself as an expert in your industry and establish your brand as the go-to brand for what you are providing,

Jefa in Training

and you will do that by integrating thought leadership into your content marketing strategy.

Make Jefa Moves by Developing Thought Leadership

Thought leadership as a practice is a way for people to see that you have the experience to sell whatever you're selling and pitch whatever you're pitching. The goal of developing your thought leadership is to have people automatically associate what you are good at with your name.

For example, when we think of the one and only AOC, US Congresswoman Alexandria Ocasio-Cortez, we know exactly what she stands for because she is a strong advocate for what she believes in and how she wants to make change.

As you get ready to launch your business, here are some ways to pave your path to becoming a thought leader:

Thought Leadership 101—A Checklist

- ☐ **Clean up your bio**. Make sure that your bios on your website, social media, and networking platforms all match. Clearly state what the bulk of the work that you do is, and be specific about the fields in which you are an expert.

- ☐ **Define what your expertise is**. Always have one or two topics in your back pocket about which you can talk for hours.

- ☐ **Set up Google Alerts** and follow other industry leaders to stay on top of industry developments—and share your thoughts on the updates with your followers.

- [ ] **Always have case studies on hand**—the more relevant, the better. Can you name people who have bought your products or worked with you as your client who can vouch for you? Be sure to share their pain points and how you helped solve them. If they are able to write a testimonial for you to share, even better.

- [ ] **Master the art of networking**. Identify where your prospects hang out, and go there. If you are hoping to sell to Latinas, join some Latina-focused communities, interact on other Latina brands' social media, and connect with other Latinas on LinkedIn. The more you talk to people, the more you will not only get out there, but the more you will also become comfortable talking through your pitch.

- [ ] **Use the soft sell method**. Thought leadership is not about pushing products or services onto people, it is about being intentional about what you say and how you say it. Here are three tips for communicating your expertise:

  - [ ] Use storytelling so people will relate to you.

  - [ ] Be as genuinely helpful as possible when people reach out with questions.

  - [ ] Provide free content. Don't be afraid of sharing too much at first, because only a handful of people will take that free content and use it as opposed to hiring you instead.

Key Takeaways from Lección 10

- You are becoming an entrepreneur and founder, but getting people to trust you and to see you as an authority in your industry is another matter—reputation is something you have to build as you build your business.

- When things get difficult, remember to stick to your "why." Hold yourself accountable just as you hold others accountable. Develop a thick skin when it comes to unconstructive criticism. Let people in and be open to feedback.

- To deal with excessive perfectionism and other challenges, start small, know you don't have to go it alone, and set boundaries.

- To be a thought leader, you must demonstrate that you are an expert at what you do in your industry. Define your area of expertise, have relevant case studies on hand, and develop your networking skills.

¡Manos a La Obra!

Developing Thought Leadership—Un Ejercicio

This ejercicio is designed to help you develop the content you will use to establish yourself as a thought leader in your industry. Whether you're launching your business tomorrow or in three months or even a year from now, it is never too soon to start presenting yourself as a thought leader.

WHAT IS YOUR EXPERTISE?

Name three to five topics for which you want to be known for being an expert. These will be the topics you post about on social media and the subjects you will use to create lead magnets. Any other content you will share will be around these topics. For example, your topics could be:

- Social Media Marketing

- Being a Latina in Tech

- Starting a side hustle and turning it into a full-time business

---

WHAT DO YOU STAND FOR?

Aside from skills and experience that you are able to share, you can share values or causes that you feel strongly about. For example, did you start your business to help crush the wage gap? Or does your business give back to a certain organization because you have a personal tie to the cause?

WHAT WOULD YOU LIKE TO BE KNOWN FOR?

Drawing from my own experience, here is an example: "Expert in community building, launching businesses, and being a woman in male-dominated fields. I care about creating equality in entrepreneurship and the arts, creating and sharing opportunities with diverse founders and artists, and giving to nonprofits that support women's health."

Once you have decided what those topics are, here are some examples of how you can start putting together a plan to establish thought leadership:

- Write, write, write! If you are comfortable writing, you can start by posting educational articles around these topics, in addition to response pieces to articles that are already out there.

- Repost. If there are articles already out there and you don't want to write a long-form response, you can repost it and highlight the points that resonate with you. If you're doing this, be sure to let the original authors know you are posting by tagging!

- Pitch yourself as a speaker—you can start by hosting webinars for like-minded communities, offering to appear on panels, connecting with universities, and for your next step—creating a TED talk!

- There are many more things you can do, like write a mini e-book (or even an actual book!), develop a course, or align yourself with a nonprofit organization that needs help with what you offer.

Buena suerte!

"A darle
que es
mole de olla."

Lección 11

Échale Ganas

"When you don't see yourself fairly represented, you understand early on that you have two choices moving forward. #1 is to embrace the emulator mindset, a fancy name for looking around to see what everyone like you is doing and setting your future goals based on other people's past results. You want to emulate *their* achievements...
The other option is to embrace the pioneer spirit; you look around to see how everyone else like you is doing, and then you open yourself up to doing something no one like you has done before...you open yourself up to the possibility of being a pioneer. And because you cannot see out there in the world what you're looking for, your guidance has to come from inside."

—Gaby Natale, Emmy Award winner, author, and entrepreneur

If we do not see people who look like us or grew up like us out there doing what we hope to one day do, we have to let that discomfort motivate us to be what we can't see. This is how we will ultimately change and make an impact for future generations. As Gaby says, sometimes we must be first so that we can move the world forward.

However, it's not always easy being a pioneer, an emprendedora, una jefa. You will have to wear many hats, and sometimes that also means finding the balance between being passionately ambitious and overworked. Other times, it will mean facing obstacles—sometimes caused by things that are beyond our control. So how do we overcome obstacles like imposter syndrome and burnout, all while trying to build our businesses? That is what we will explore in this chapter.

A Guide to Staying Brava

There are certain fears that can come with the new experience of being a jefa, especially for first-generation Latinas or children of immigrants. As an immigrant, Gaby Natale feared speaking in public when she first arrived in America because she spoke with an accent. Gaby's story is just one of many that can inspire us all to be pioneers and go on to create more space in industries where we may not normally be represented.

At some point along your entrepreneurial journey, you may be faced with a situation where you are feeling a bit out of your comfort zone— maybe because you're the only woman in the room or the only person of color in the room, or perhaps because it's your first time doing what you're about to do. You may be experiencing "imposter syndrome," and here are some tools to get you through it.

Para Más Inspiración: Unos Consejos

Four Ways to Slay Imposter Syndrome from Melba Tellez

Imposter syndrome is defined by the Harvard Business Review as "the collection of feelings of inadequacy that persist despite evident success." Even after working so hard and knowing we deserve every opportunity that comes our way, the feeling creeps in. As a leading Latina in tech and the founder of Mujeres on the Rise, a platform that connects Latina women and provides them with resources and tools to grow their careers, Melba Tellez shares how she tackles this feeling.

✧ **Be open and honest about how you are feeling:**
There is great power in vulnerability, and when you're facing imposter syndrome, I find it helpful to share this with others who are supportive, whether it be a mentor, a friend, or a colleague. In doing so, you'll often find that you are not alone. You'll also likely be met with great advice by someone who has "been there and done that."

✧ **No one can do what you do the way you do it.**
Remember: It's important that we don't compare ourselves to other people. In the end, each of us is here for a reason and there is room for all of us to grow and succeed.

✧ **Seek community:** When I was younger there weren't many resources or communities specifically for Latina women. Now there are so many, and I honestly love seeing it. When things get hard, it's great to have people you can rely on for encouragement.

✧ **Keep track of your accomplishments and accolades:**
It can be hard to remember our value, so I highly recommend keeping tabs on your achievements, awards, promotions, peer accolades, and everything in between! The moment you begin to doubt yourself, pull those resources out, take a good look at them, and remind yourself that you are deserving of every opportunity, every promotion, every raise—all of it!

You are in that room for a reason. If you are feeling imposter syndrome, remember this: the reason that imposter syndrome exists is because more people like you aren't doing what they want to do. By doing what you fear, you're breaking the cycle.

Become a Time Management Master

One of the most common pain points for new entrepreneurs who are building their businesses while still working a full-time job is figuring out how to manage their time. Even when you are working on your business full-time, this is still a skill you will need to master to be able to efficiently get through all the tasks you need to do each day.

Everyone has techniques they use, and any specific technique may work better for some people than it does for others, so here are three different methods; try implementing them this week and see how you feel!

THE EISENHOWER MATRIX FOR DAILY AND WEEKLY PLANNING

Time management is not just about setting certain times to do things, it is also about knowing how to prioritize tasks. The Eisenhower Matrix was developed to help you do that! Created by Dwight D. Eisenhower, the thirty-fourth president of the United States, it is used to prioritize tasks by how urgent or important they are. This is done by filling in a chart with four quadrants like the one on the next page.

Jefa in Training

Important/Urgent	Important/ Not Urgent

Not Important/Urgent	Not Important/ Not Urgent

On the top left, list the things you have to do for the day that are both most urgent and most important to you. These will be the tasks you will do immediately after planning—here you would include the tasks which have immediate deadlines for completion. In the next quadrant, write to-do items that are less urgent but still important—perhaps longer-term planning activities and/or personal errands. Then you will schedule time slots to do these things, either later that same day or later in the week. For the bottom left quadrant, list the tasks that are urgent, yet not so important. These are tasks that you could delegate to someone to do for you to get off them your plate—this could include necessary research for a future project, ordering groceries, or scheduling social media

posts. Lastly, the fourth quadrant is where you can leave tasks that can just be skipped altogether.

THE POMODORO TECHNIQUE TO IMPROVE DAILY PRODUCTIVITY

The Pomodoro Technique was developed in the 1980s by a student named Francesco Cirillo who was struggling to focus on his assignments. This technique's strength is its simplicity; just set a timer and work on tasks in bursts of time. If you think this can work for you, here is a sample schedule for you to try!

▶ Start with a to-do list for the day.

▶ Pick a task (e.g., content planning for next month).

▶ Set a timer for twenty-five minutes.

▶ Do a task for that time.

▶ Take a five-minute break.

▶ Repeat two or three times.

▶ Take a thirty-minute break.

▶ Repeat!

TIME-BLOCKING: SEPARATE TASKS BY DAY OR TIME

For those of us balancing many projects at once, time-blocking (aka batching) is a great way to focus on one project for a certain block of time. For example, Mondays from six to eight o'clock could be your social media content planning time, Tuesdays from ten o'clock to noon might be your regular writing time, and so on.

Here is how you can start:

▶ Open up your favorite planner—paper, digital, or both!

▶ Write out the hours in your workday on a lined page (if your planner does not already have labeled blanks for your workday hours). Example:

Monday
9 a.m.
10 a.m.
11 a.m.

▶ Block off windows of time for each type of task you have to get done. If you are working on multiple projects, you can also schedule different projects on different days. For example, Mondays and Wednesdays can be your client-focused days, Thursdays and Saturdays can be your writing days, and Fridays could be for administrative tasks.

Evaluate How You Use Your Time

It's important to evaluate how you use your time each week and see how it lines up with your weekly goals. For example, if your main goal was to increase your sales by 25 percent this month, and you only spent 25 percent of your time this week working on implementing your marketing and sales strategy, that's not ideal. If you know that you only have fifteen hours a week to spend on your business, break those hours up based on the priorities that must be accomplished for you to reach your goals. Make a pie chart for the month if it is helpful!

Tracking your own time is just as important as tracking your leads, sales, and expenses!

Balancing It All

Being the best jefa you can be requires more than a good business model and the right mindset—it also requires balance. The abilities to prioritize tasks and manage your time effectively are just pieces of the puzzle. Everyone needs to take breaks—schedule them into your planner if you must, but make sure they happen. According to an article by Meg Selig in *Psychology Today*, breaks can prevent "decision fatigue," restore motivation, and increase productivity and creativity, as well as improve memory and learning.

Failure to take breaks can result in burnout—the kind of emotional and physical exhaustion that leaves you feeling like you just want to quit everything. Knowing when to take some time off or even when to temporarily walk away from a task is a leadership skill. You will not be able to grow if you consistently drive yourself into overwhelm.

Para Más Inspiración: Unos Consejos

Five Tips for Dealing with Burnout from Cat Lantigua

Along with working long hours, feeling stuck, and/or feeling unfulfilled, women often experience burnout more rapidly and more often because of microaggressions they face in professional settings, as well as being underpaid and/or constantly compared to white men.

Cat Lantigua, podcast host and founder of Goddess Council, a wellness community for women seeking connections and healing, started her business because she was experiencing loneliness and depression due to the pressures of living in New York City. Now, the community she has

Jefa in Training

built serves as a digital space where women can show up fully and have meaningful conversations.

As an advocate for wellness, Cat knows how important it is to incorporate it into your entrepreneurial journey. As she says, "[Wellness] just simply has to be integrated. This isn't about adding in meditation sessions or baths and calling it a day. It is starting from a place of 'you deserve to be treated well by yourself.' You need to believe you are worthy of care. You need to believe that the version of you who builds this business into a success happens to be the same version of you who takes good care of yourself."

Identifying Burnout

Burning out is subtle; it doesn't just happen from one day to the next, it builds up over time. You slowly drain your battery day after day, but on any given day, you probably wouldn't say you are burnt out. It's hard to tell when you are going through it, but eventually, your battery gets so low that you can no longer function, and that's when you finally realize you are experiencing burnout. Burnout can be prevented by becoming more aware of the habits and patterns that drain you, as well as doing what you can to recharge.

Remember to prioritize yourself over your business.

Admittedly, I'm not great at this, but I am getting there! Building a business has many moving parts, and it feels like there is always more work to be done, but this can trap us into prioritizing the business over our own wellbeing. Which *kind of* makes sense—it's your business! There are things that need to be done, and while you may need to do them, if you aren't filling your own cup first, then everything will eventually suffer—that includes both you and your business. You and your mental, physical, and emotional health need to come before the business if you want your endeavor to succeed (especially if you want to build your dream while holding onto your sanity).

Build a routine. It takes time to build new habits, but eventually, working your way up to having some of your self-care built into every day helps with maintaining better overall health. Creating and sticking to a clarifying morning routine to get in the zone and then an intentional routine at night to wind down and relax can really work wonders, especially over time. Start by phasing in one new activity until it is actually a habit, then add something else. Remember, Rome wasn't built in a day.

Schedule time for play and adventure. Find a block of a few hours in your calendar where you can go for a hike, color, go dancing, or whatever it is that gets your inner child excited. Even if you are in a soul-aligned business, the work can be draining, and we aren't robots. We are still just kids who want to play, and we shouldn't forget that. Yes, you have big hopes and dreams, but you also deserve a break—a *real* break.

Enter airplane mode. You do not have to be accessible to everyone all the time. Set boundaries with the outside world so you can recharge and tap back into who you are and what you need in this moment. The world will still be there when you get back, I promise.

Take as long as you need. It took you a while to get into this state, and it may take you a while to get out of it. Be gentle with yourself. Be kind to yourself. You *aren't* a robot! Even if there is a lot to do, what you need right now is to be a good friend to yourself, not a demanding boss.

No Estas Sola

When I first launched #WCM, I burned myself out time and time again—not because I felt unfulfilled or worked 24/7, but because I got wrapped up in my own thoughts and fears to such a degree that I started letting doubt cripple the growth of the organization. I now see that this could have been avoided sooner had I let someone in to be my mentor. Having a personal board of advisors to consult with twice a year is great, but having someone to provide ongoing mentorship is *gold*.

Good mentors will be there for you, providing advice and support to help you through any changes or challenges you face. They differ from your advisors both in how often you will connect with them and in the way they provide value to your business. They may be more open to telling you about their personal experiences as well as more willing to give you strategic advice.

To find a mentor, look to your professional and personal circle. Do you keep in touch with an old boss? Do you have a family member or family friend who has been a support for you in the past? Is there a thought leader you follow who is open to being a mentor?

You may find that you will need more than one mentor or that you will outgrow certain mentors depending on what phase of your life and career you are in, and that's okay. Keep in touch with the people who have inspired you, opened doors for you, and always seen potential in you. That is how mentor-mentee relationships begin, and you never know what resources they could provide you in the future. You do not have to be alone on this new path you are on!

- If you are experiencing imposter syndrome, remember this: The reason that imposter syndrome exists is because more people like you aren't doing what they want to do. By doing what makes you afraid or anxious, you are breaking the cycle.

- Keep track of your accomplishments and accolades! The moment you begin to doubt yourself, pull out those resources and remind yourself that you are deserving of every promotion, raise, and opportunity.

- Knowing when to take some time off or even temporarily walk away from a task is a leadership skill. You will not be able to grow if you consistently drive yourself into overwhelm.

- Wellness simply *must* be integrated into your journey. This isn't about adding in some meditation sessions or baths and calling it a day. It is starting from a place of knowing you deserve to be treated well by yourself. You need to believe you are worthy of care.

- To find a mentor, look to your professional and personal circle. Keep in touch with those who have opened doors for you in the past.

¡Manos a La Obra!

Defining Your Leadership

Think about leaders in your industry that you admire. Who are they and why do you follow them? How do they present themselves that makes you feel inspired? What other emotions do they trigger when you are reading their books, scrolling their posts, or looking at their achievements?

As you start building your brand, you will also start developing your own leadership style. What do you want your life as a jefa to look like? What do you want people to say about you? For this ejercicio, we are going to do a visualization exercise.

Visualize yourself three years from now and answer the following:

▶ What do you want your community to be saying about you?

▶ What are your strengths?

▶ Do you delegate enough?

▶ How do you balance your time?

▶ Do you still have the same doubts about your business as you do today?

_____

_____

_____

_____

_____

Start becoming this kind of leader today. Create and prioritize your schedule, become more aware of how you spend your time, and confront your doubts and fears by letting people in to help. ¡Y a lo que sigue, que ya casi estas lista!

"Poco a poco se anda lejos."

Lección 12

Disfrutando el Camino

From developing your idea to mapping your customer journey, crafting your Unique Selling Proposition, and learning how to establish yourself as a thought leader, you've made it to la ultima lección. The title is "Disfrutando el Camino" because after all the planning and preparation, the only thing left to do is let go of the what-ifs and enjoy the journey you're about to start.

In this chapter, we will go through a checklist of prelaunch to-dos, as well as some tips for after your launch, and we'll hear from some other Latina entrepreneurs on mistakes to avoid. But before we go into all of this, I want you to acknowledge how far you have come since Lección 1. Maybe you started with a tiny idea, or maybe you started with no idea at all—and now it has become the beginning of something great. You have put in the work to start it, now it's time to let it flourish.

Before You Launch

A great way to prepare for the actual launch of your business is to do a *soft launch*. A soft launch is when you open your business to a limited number of people, a customer group available for you to test your products and services. These customers will be your *beta test group*. During your soft launch, you can collect feedback and start to see what processes are effective, what you might be missing, and what you may need to change.

You can reach out to the people you spoke to during your initial market research phase, and if you want to create some buzz, you can announce through your marketing that you'll be doing an "invite only" launch and have people apply to be part of your beta phase.

The length of your beta phase is up to you. The important part is that you collect relevant data that will allow you to cover your bases before opening the doors to a larger audience. For some launches, the beta phase may be three months; for others, it can be a year. You will determine what data will matter the most to you during this time, but here are some important questions to consider:

- Is your product and/or service effectively serving customers' needs, or do you need to tweak your offerings?

- Is your Unique Selling Proposition made clear in all of your marketing materials? Are prospective customers getting a full vision of your brand when they learn about you?

- What is your customer experience like? From onboarding through the end of the process, is it a smooth flow? How are they responding to retention efforts?

- Are your processes set up so that you are able to take on more customers? Can you see your enterprise being scalable?

- What are people saying about working with you? What needs to be improved before concluding the beta phase?

You can use a soft launch to collect testimonials and reviews, as well as identify who your potential ambassadors are. It can also give you time to keep improving on your marketing and other processes, and fine-tuning your product or service. However, your soft launch should not be the first time you analyze your business and marketing approach. That should be done before you launch your research phase in case what you learn means you need to completely restart from scratch. Your products for your soft launch should be the ones you already know

work; you just want to discover exactly *how* they meet the needs of your customers.

Your Launch Checklist

While everyone's timeline may be different in terms of how long they take to launch, the roadmap is the same. Here is a checklist for you based on the previous chapters and exercises. Go through each of these and see if you've missed anything.

- ❑ Business name
- ❑ Mission and vision defined
- ❑ Target audience
- ❑ Initial market research complete
- ❑ Registered with your state
- ❑ Business bank account opened
- ❑ Financial plan and budget set
- ❑ Website and social media handles created
- ❑ Unique Selling Proposition identified
- ❑ Pitch fine-tuned until it's solid
- ❑ Buyer personas identified
- ❑ Customer journey mapped out

- ❑ Lead magnets created
- ❑ Marketing content planned
- ❑ Press release and media list ready to go
- ❑ Partnerships created to spread the word
- ❑ Referral/affiliate system set up
- ❑ Thought leadership content created, as well as other thought leaders in your industry followed
- ❑ Google Alerts for industry news set up
- ❑ Next quarter planned out
- ❑ Soft launch
- ❑ Celebrate your wins!

Adelante!

What to Expect Post-Launch

After you have launched, feel proud of yourself, but also know there is work ahead—this is just the beginning. After your first quarter in business, do a new SWOT Analysis to see where the gaps might be in your initial plan. You may encounter the following issues:

You're Not Reaching Your Target Audience

If you find you are not reaching enough of the right people, it could be a sign that you need to more narrowly define your target niche. Sometimes, if you set your target audience to a large group of people, it can make things easier to start with a smaller target group. For example, if your initial target audience was women aged eighteen to thirty-five, perhaps you'd want to start by hitting the twenty-five to thirty-five demographic first, and so you'd adjust your marketing and sales strategy to reflect that. While that is a smaller group of people, if you can capture the attention of more twenty-five- to thirty-five-year-old women with your strategies versus being spread too thin to attract all of the eighteen-to-thirty-five-year-old female demographic, you'll be engaging more of the right people.

You're Getting Attention, But Leads Are Not Converting

If you are getting website views and newsletter subscriptions but no one is taking the next step into your marketing funnel, there could be a couple of things to consider. The first is this: Is your Unique Selling Proposition clear and present in your outreach in a way that cannot be

Jefa in Training

missed? It could be that your Unique Selling Proposition has possibly gotten lost, so people aren't understanding what makes you different and what value you could bring to them. The second is that maybe your Click Through Rate is just not high enough yet. Do your website pages have enough call-to-action buttons? (Buttons offering actions like "shop here" or "sign up here," for example.) Are you losing their attention too early in your funnel? Redo your customer journey map to see where you can add or edit steps!

Your Sales Are Not Covering Your Expenses

While it is normal that most small businesses will not turn a profit in the first two to three years of business, you should analyze your cash flow if you are seeing a very large amount of money going out of your business and not as much coming in. Go back to your financial plan and see if you need to buy less inventory, raise your prices, or temporarily cut down on software or packaging costs. If you need a quick boost in revenue, a flash sale may help your short-term cash flow and increase your reach to new customers.

You're Offering Too Much

Whether you have a service- or product-based business, it is possible to offer too much to the client. In an effort to be more accessible to different clients or to provide flexibility in what we offer, sometimes we do more than we ourselves can keep up with, and it isn't worth it if it's not helping us scale. If you are a team of one for now, only add on things that you are sure you can handle. Until those things start taking off and you can afford to add on not only the cost of more product or service offerings

but the cost of someone to help you with them, hold off! It's not a race. Remember: you're going for building a sustainable business.

You Don't Feel Aligned with What You're Building

It happens sometimes, but before you give up on your current enterprise and move on to your next idea, consider shifting your business model instead. Is this something that isn't working as a business, but that you think could get sponsor attention as a nonprofit? Could you offer a subscription service versus charging a one-time upfront fee? Is your pricing too divergent from that of your competitors?

If you don't think your business model itself needs a pivot but you're starting to lose passion, that's okay. If you're not seeing a demand for your business (and maybe it's been over a month since you've had a warm lead), or if there's no buzz around the brand and you find yourself apologizing on behalf of the business time and time again, then it might be time to walk away. The important thing is that you learn from your experience: Was your idea based on a seasonal trend? Did you find an industry with which you feel more in alignment?

Change Can Be Good—and It's Necessary

"Si el plan no funciona, cambia el plan, pero no cambies la meta." If you do feel that it's time to walk away from your original idea, it might be time to plan a pivot—but it won't be a complete redo, as the personal "why" driving you will still be at the center of your efforts.

Industries are constantly changing, and the things you'll learn along your journey may also prompt you to want to change things within your business. As business owners, we must be flexible and evolve just as the world evolves. To develop your business, change is necessary. Whether it's an expansion or a pivot in direction, it's not a step backward, it's a step toward growth.

Lessons Learned

This is all a learning experience, and we will all make mistakes at some point along the way. This is a normal part of the process that we can use to grow and build better processes and businesses. Some of my collaborators have shared their missteps to help you either avoid similar situations or move past them.

Do Not Wait for Everything to Be Perfect

"I thought that I needed to have everything perfect before launching The Mujerista. I had a list of things I wanted, which all took time, and it kept delaying the launch. Looking back, I think I was using not having certain things ready as an excuse to not launch—out of fear. The things I wanted were not needed for my launch, and I lost a lot of time. Sometimes we just have to take the leap!"

—Marivette Navarrete, founder of The Mujerista

Push Through and Don't Get Discouraged

"When I was first starting out, I had big dreams for what
the community [I was starting] could be, so when reality
fell short of my dreams, it was easy to get discouraged. I
had many fully packed events at my apartment in the early
days (between ten and fifteen people). But I also had events
where three people showed up or none at all, and those
moments felt overwhelming. When your idea is so young
and most of it still exists in your head, those little reality
checks can be hard to stomach. I think we all go through
it in the early days, and there is not necessarily a clear
antidote. It feels uncomfortable and confusing, but you have
to push through and stay connected with your vision for
your business. Those reality checks can also be important
because we can learn from our shortcomings, but they
aren't reasons to give up, even though they may feel like it
at the time."

—Cat Lantigua, founder of Goddess Council

Do Not Try to Be Like Others

"Being *you* is your most valuable tool; my mistake at first was trying to run a business by fitting in. Cadena really took off when I embraced my culture and lived experiences. For so long I was trying to blend in. Running Cadena Collective taught me to show up as my authentic self and to celebrate my culture. This included the way I dressed and the things I was speaking up about. Speaking on who I am and where I came from gave me an edge because we don't celebrate enough stories about first-generation Latinas who have overcome great odds to be successful. I am proud to show up with a bold red lip, my rizos, and my statement earrings. Calladita no more!"

—Alejandra Aguirre, founder of Cadena Collective

You Don't Have to Choose Between Profit and Purpose

"When I first started my business, I was offering free resume consultations and career coaching. That's right, anyone that approached me would receive my services 100 percent free. The funny thing is that on social media, I'm very vocal about my stance on equal pay, and I encourage women to always seek their worth. One day, a friend kindly pointed out that I was not doing that—and he was right. I could not teach self-advocacy without practicing it myself. Soon after, I put together a pricing sheet and started promoting my services.

"As an entrepreneur, that experience taught me that you don't have to pick between profit and purpose. You can make money while making a difference. I have since learned to balance free resources and tips with paid services. I also donate 10 percent of proceeds to nonprofit organizations that support women in need."

—Melba Tellez, founder of Mujeres on the Rise

Don't Be Afraid to Break the Rules

As a Latina-owned, self-funded, socially conscious small business, I am constantly entering spaces where my business, Rizos Curls, is the first of its kind. It has challenged me to question the rules, break down outdated corporate norms & disrupt the industry on my path to success.

Just because something hasn't been done before doesn't mean it's not possible. Don't be afraid to do things differently. In fact, in being different is where I have found my magic.

If the playbook is there for all to see, then what makes you stand out from the competition? EVERYTHING is negotiable when you are building something truly NEW. Don't expect the same rules to apply to your business as they do to fortune 500 companies.

Spending thousands to create unauthentic content? Boring. Lacking diversity? Out of touch.

Don't do something just because it's what other brands are doing. Embrace what makes you YOU and make it part of your strategy.

—Julissa Prado, founder and CEO of Rizos Curls

Invest in Yourself

> "Don't be afraid to make smart, intentional investments—
> even before your business has made money. Remember that
> you are your business, so investing in yourself, including
> continued education, mentors, and communities, can be so
> helpful right from the beginning."
>
> —Vanessa Castillo, founder of VCV Agency and Rich
> Girl Mindset

And finally, here's one from me.

Do Not Overlook Setting Up Your Foundation

#WomxnCrush Music's community and programs grew
faster than I could have ever imagined, and while that
sounds good, it gave me very little time to create a business
plan. I completely overlooked the need to have a solid
financial and administrative foundation; so for the first year
and a half, we were running without any kind of strategic
plan. While things kept going, we were not in a position to
keep *growing*. Do the work now, because when you launch,
people will come, and you want to be ready to support them
(and yourself).

Defining What Success Means to You

Before we go on to finalize your plan, think about what success means
to you. Does it mean quitting your full-time job in the next year? Does it
mean hiring a small staff? Do you want to expand into different markets
and seek investors down the line?

Your Owner Strategy

While planning out your goals for the first year of business, you'll want to take a look at what is most important to you: growth, control, or liquidity. This is also known as your "owner strategy." According to the Harvard Business Review, in most cases, owners focus on two of those goals at the expense of the third.

Some combinations to consider are:

GROWTH AND CONTROL

This means that your business is focused on expanding while you retain control of decisions; this usually entails no outside investments, and in general paying yourself a minimal salary in order to be able to keep investing in the business so you can to offer more products and/or services.

LIQUIDITY AND CONTROL

This strategic choice means that regardless of growth, for you, cash flow is the top priority. You still want to be the sole owner of your business to keep your decision-making power, and you will limit how much you can offer in order to make the most profit.

LIQUIDITY AND GROWTH

When companies go public, this is what they are focused on. This means they are giving up equity in order to be able to expand the business further. Generally, if it is a very competitive market and you need to see growth fast, this would be your priority.

✳   ✳   ✳

With these values in mind, think about your goals for your first year, then for the first five years of your business.

With what mindset will you approach your first year?

_____

_____

What will your focus be from years two to five?

_____

_____

As you're getting ready to embark on this new chapter of your life, remember that your journey will likely not be linear—and that is normal. That means that if you have to spend three more months on market research than planned, that's okay. If you need to test your product for longer before you can do a soft launch, that's okay. If you need to consult various mentors before implementing a new idea after you've launched, that's also okay. Remember that this book is a roadmap and a toolkit, not a rule book. You have frameworks, you've read about others' experiences and knowledge, and now it's your turn to implement all of it however you see that it fits your values, your life, and the foundation for the business you have created.

Now there is only one thing left to do, jefa!

Key Takeaways from Lección 12

▶ A great way to prepare for the actual launch of your business is to do a soft launch. During your soft launch, you can collect feedback and start to see what processes are effective, what you might be missing, and what you may need to change.

▶ Once you have launched, feel proud of yourself, but also know there is work ahead. This is just the beginning. After your first quarter in business, do a new SWOT Analysis to see where the gaps might be in your initial plan.

▶ "Si el plan no funciona, cambia el plan, pero no cambies la meta." If you do feel that it's time to walk away from your original idea, it might be time to plan a pivot—but it won't be a complete redo, as the personal "why" driving you will still be at the center of your choices.

▶ Don't wait for everything to be perfect, and don't get discouraged. Don't be afraid to invest in yourself. Remember that you don't have to choose between profit and purpose, and do not overlook setting your foundation.

▶ Define your owner strategy in relation to the essential business priorities of growth, control, and liquidity.

▶ Create your one-year and five-year goals based on what success means to you.

¡Manos a La Obra!

Developing Your Business Model

You are one step away from completing the *Jefa in Training* toolkit—the very first step in launching your next entrepreneurial venture—and I can't wait to see what you create.

It is finally time we start piecing everything into one place to create your business model. The ejercicio you will do to wrap up this chapter is based on the Business Model Canvas created by Alexander Osterwalder, author of *Business Model Ontology*. The goal of this exercise is to make certain you have all the key elements of what makes up your business in place. You can of course reassess these different parts any time you see that it is needed.

DEFINING THE KEY ELEMENTS

Key Partners: These will be the people, organizations, and networks with whom you'll be working the most to roll out your business operations. Do you have suppliers? Will you be collaborating with others to host events? Who will be referring clients to you?

_____

_____

Key Activities: These are your offerings and the source of your revenue streams. Depending on what your business' stock in trade is, your key activities could include hosting events such as retreats or even summits, writing articles, selling products or templates for others to use, creating webinars, or doing one-on-one coaching or other types of sessions with clients. What are the key activities for your business?

_____

_____

Key Resources: What do you need to be able to execute these activities? Do you need a venue, funding for materials, a platform from which to sell things, and/or equipment for a sound setup?

_____

_____

Value Propositions: This is your Unique Selling Proposition! What is the value you are providing? What needs are you meeting? How do your key activities tie into the needs of your customers?

_____

_____

Customer Relationships: What is your acquisition and retention plan? Do you already have relationships with some customers?

_____

_____

Customer Segments: Who are these customers? Who is *not* going to be your customer? Include your buyer personas here.

_____

_____

Channels: How are you reaching your potential and current customers? Do your competitors reach them differently? Which ways of communication are most engaging and cost-effective?

_____

_____

Cost Structure: Do you have a lot of expenses? What are they? What are the most expensive resources you need for your business (materials, platforms, equipment, etc.)? Which activities are most expensive (retreats, summits, shipping for large products, or others)?

_____

_____

Revenue Streams: What are competitors charging for the value you provide? How do you make money? Per hour, per product, or per subscription? What method are you using to develop your pricing?

_____

_____

"Siempre cree que lo imposible es siempre posible."

-Selena Quintanilla-Pérez

Lección 13

¡Si Se Puede!

Felicidades, jefas. You made it.

There is only one thing left to do, and that is to launch!

My hope is that with this book, you now have the tools to build the foundation of your creative or entrepreneurial project. Whether you are starting the next beauty empire, your first coaching business, or an award-winning publishing company, or if you're on the road to releasing a Grammy-award winning album, or launching tech that will change people's lives—I am so proud of you.

I want you to review the chapters and worksheets as you go through your journey and redo the frameworks when you need them; and then, when you feel like you have conquered building your business foundation, pass this toolkit along to someone else. By taking the step of reading *Jefa in Training* to start your business, you've also participated in bettering the entrepreneurial landscape for women like us—and that is how we create real change.

There will be ups and downs, there will be risks and rewards, but at the end of the day, you'll feel proud of yourself for having launched something that began as only a dream of what you could do. And if I can impart one last piece of advice, it is this: Celebrate every win, big and small, starting now.

So celebrate that you have built your foundation, and then go for it—and do it fearlessly. And I'll leave you with the words mi mami has always said to me:

"¡Si se puede!"

—Laura S. Ojeda

Adelante, jefas! A whole new world awaits you.

XOXO,
Ashley K. Stoyanov Ojeda

"Más sabe el diablo por viejo que por diablo."

Para Seguirle

This book may be ending, but the training of an emprendedora is never done. This is a reminder to always stay in the loop with new trends in your industry and new collaborators that may pop up. Not only should you be alert to what will lift up your business, but as a jefa, you should always be learning.

Here are some tips on how to be a life-long estudiante:

- If you haven't already done so, set up Google alerts for keywords in your industry.

- Subscribe to relevant newsletters.

- Take classes and webinars to always be leveling up.

- Listen to podcasts or read books by other powerhouses in your industry to stay inspired.

- Join an online or IRL community with like-minded people, to both keep you on track and stay involved in current discussions in your field.

And lastly, here's a list of other recommended books you may find helpful on your camino to embracing your new journey as a business owner. This list has been created con mucho amor with help from the jefas featured in the book.

Libros

Big Magic: Creative Living Beyond Fear by Elizabeth Gilbert. (Riverhead Books / Penguin Random House, New York, 2015.)

Building a StoryBrand: Clarify Your Message So Customers Will Listen by Donald Miller. (HarperCollins Leadership / HarperCollins Focus, New York, 2017.)

Dare to Lead: Brave Work. Tough Conversations. Whole Hearts. by Brené Brown. (Random House, New York, 2018.)

Do Cool Sh*t: Quit Your Day Job, Start Your Own Business, and Live Happily Ever After by Miki Agrawal. (HarperBusiness, New York, 2013.)

Drop the Ball: Achieving More by Doing Less by Tiffany Dufu. (Flatiron Books, New York, 2017.)

The E-Myth Revisited: Why Most Small Businesses Don't Work and What to Do About It by Michael E. Gerber. (HarperBusiness, New York, 1995, 2001, 2004.)

Emergent Strategy: Shaping Change, Changing Worlds by adrienne maree brown. (AK Press, Chico, California, 2017.)

Girl Code: Unlocking the Secrets to Success, Sanity, & Happiness for the Female Entrepreneur by Cara Alwill Leyba. (Penguin Books Ltd., 2015.)

How to Win Friends & Influence People by Dale Carnegie. (Pocket Books / Simon & Schuster, New York, 1936, 1964, 1998.)

Jefa in Training

It's About Damn Time: How to Turn Being Underestimated Into Your Greatest Advantage by Arlan Hamilton with Rachel L. Nelson. (Currency / Penguin Random House, New York, 2020.)

Ladies Get Paid: The Ultimate Guide to Breaking Barriers, Owning Your Worth, and Taking Command of Your Career by Claire Wasserman. (Gallery Books / Simon & Schuster, New York, 2021.)

Lead the Field by Earl Nightingale. (BN Publishing, Hawthorne, California, 2007.)

Leapfrog: The New Revolution for Women Entrepreneurs by Nathalie Molina Niño with Sara Grace. (TarcherPerigee / Penguin Random House, New York, 2018.)

The Memo: What Women of Color Need to Know to Secure a Seat at the Table by Minda Harts. (Seal Press / Hachette Book Group, New York, 2020.)

Profit First: Transform Your Business from a Cash-Eating Monster to a Money-Making Machine by Mike Michalowicz. (Gildan Media, Flushing, New York, 2017.)

Self Made: Becoming Empowered, Self-Reliant, and Rich in Every Way by Nely Galán. (Spiegel & Grau / Penguin Random House, New York, 2016.)

Start With Why: How Great Leaders Inspire Everyone to Take Action by Simon Sinek. (Portfolio / Penguin Group, New York, 2009.)

The Virtuous Circle: Restore Your Confidence, Bounce Back, and Emerge Stronger by Gaby Natale. (HarperCollins Leadership / HarperCollins Focus, New York, 2021.)

Traction: Get A Grip on Your Business by Gino Wickman. (BenBella Books, Dallas, Texas, 2011.)

You Are a Badass [series] by Jen Sincero. (John Murray Learning, London, UK, 2013.)

Acknowledgements
¡Muchas Gracias a Todos!

Writing a book was always on my bucket list, but *Jefa In Training* is about so much more than checking off a to-do. It is about sharing experiences and knowledge to empower other women with similar life paths to not be afraid to build something for themselves. It is about creating change and cultivating opportunities in spaces where we feel like we don't fit in. It's about embracing our cultura and using what makes us diferente to do something no one has done before.

Without Mango Publishing, this would not have been possible, so my first thank you goes out to them. Jessica Faroy, Yaddyra Peralta, and Jackie Sousa, muchas gracias for believing in me since el día numero uno. You are the best team I could have dreamed up to help this book come to life.

To all the collaborators in these chapters: Stephanie and Melissa Carcache, Tania Torres, Vanessa Castillo, Lila Miller, Jackie Garcia-Arteaga, Vanessa Duran, Reyna Marrufo, Paulette Pinero, Melba Torres, Cat Lantigua, Ana Flores, Danielle Alvarez, Vivian Nunez, Marilyn La Jeunesse—thank you so much for sharing your knowledge with me to inspire the jefas in training and pave the way for more of us to shine.

To my husband, Martin: you have believed in every single one of my business ideas, pivots, and spontaneous decisions, and supported me every step of the way. Thank you for always going the extra mile to make sure I can live out my dreams. Te amo.

To my parents:

- Dad, from attending every bar gig, to reading all my articles, to sharing all of my wins on Facebook—thank you for always telling me to keep shooting for the stars, and for being there watching me do it all.

- Mami, muchas gracias por siempre creer en mí y por siempre recordarme que si, si se puede. Eres mi mayor inspiración— gracias por enseñarme a ser líder. No sería la mitad de la jefa que soy hoy sin tus consejos y tu apoyo.

A mi hermano Diego: thank you for always having my back and inspiring me to keep pushing through.

A mis primos en Mexico, Marlene and Juanfra: thank you for being such a huge influence in my life, and for being there since I started writing at fifteen.

To my mother-in-law Natalia and my sister-in-law Ellen: thank you for always believing in me!

And of course, a mis abuelitas (RIP), Denise y Rosalina: this book would not exist without you.

A las jefas de la Mujerista: thank you for literally everything.

Marivette: thank you for changing my life by trusting me to help build your brainchild and for being una gran amiga.

Jefa in Training

Lis: I don't even know where to start—thank you for being my therapist, makeup artist, and everything in between. I would be lost without you.

Yovana, my greatest mentee and amiga: your support and creativity has helped so much during this process!

To my volunteers at #WomxnCrush Music: you all are the hardest-working team and make me so proud to be a founder.

To my mentors:

- Matt Eyman, thank you for your ongoing support, for everything you've taught me, and for giving me a chance all those years ago.

- Daniel Friedland, thank you for trusting me in growing your space and, without knowing it, giving me the inspiration to start writing this book.

- Nidhi Doshi and Rajeev Prasad, thank you for trusting me with building your business and inspiring me to be a better leader and changemaker.

- Claire Wasserman, thank you for being such a huge help on my journey as a first-time author! Your guidance has been so appreciated!

And last but not least: to the entrepreneurial badasses for being the ongoing inspiration behind this book—my clients. Thank you for trusting me to help build your empires and for being there for me when I need you.

Muchas, muchas gracias a todos. We did it.

About the Author

Ashley K. Stoyanov Ojeda is a community-builder, business-development strategist, coach, and socialpreneur. Originally from Queens, NYC, and born to a Mexican mom and French-American father, Ashley's career started in the music industry in 2012, working at major record labels, publishers, and venues. After relocating to Portland, OR, post-college, she created her own network for local womxn songwriters, now a national organization that has been featured in The Recording Academy, called #WomxnCrush Music.

Since the rapid growth of her organization, she has dedicated her career to creating opportunities and developing businesses and communities of underrepresented entrepreneurs through her coaching and consulting, and has become known as the Business Hada Madrina (Business Fairygodmother).

Ashley joined The Mujerista team in 2020 to help create and grow The Mujerista Network, a digital network dedicated to empowering and celebrating the next generation of Latinas making an impact en la cultura. Ashley currently resides in Portland, Oregon.

FLORIDA INTERNATIONAL UNIVERSITY

FIU Business Press equips professionals with the essential tools and skills for business success in a rapidly evolving world. An imprint of Mango Publishing, FIU Business Press is part of Florida International University's College of Business, a top-ranked school by U.S. News & World Report. The college has been recognized as the nation's #2 international business program, #8 international MBA, and #22 online master's in business. Based in Miami, FIU has been named a top-50 innovative public university and is the nation's fourth largest university with a student body of more than 54,000.

Mango Publishing, which publishes an eclectic list of books by diverse authors, was named 2019 and 2020's #1 fastest growing independent publisher by Publishers Weekly. Through a partnership of FIU College of Business office of Executive Education and Mango Publishing, FIU Business Press shares innovative, yet practical, business knowledge that allows professionals and executives to thrive globally.

Help us fuel business growth by sharing your thoughts and ideas:

Read about FIU's business programs:
business.fiu.edu/executive-education
Email us: FiuExecEd@fiu.edu
Follow us on LinkedIn: Florida International University-College of BusinessFIU Executive Education
Newsletter: mangopublishinggroup.com/newsletter

CPSIA information can be obtained
at www.ICGtesting.com
Printed in the USA
JSHW050048090222
22659JS00006B/9